Listening to the Animals

ONE OF
THE FAMILY

EDITED BY PHYLLIS HOBE

A GUIDEPOSTS BOOK

ACKNOWLEDGMENTS

Every attempt has been made to credit the sources of copyrighted material used in this book. If any such acknowledgment has been inadvertently omitted or miscredited, receipt of such information would be appreciated.

All material that originally appeared in *Guideposts* magazine, *Angels on Earth* or *Daily Guideposts* is reprinted with permission. Copyright © 1982, 1986, 1991, 1993, 1995, 1998, 1999.

"The St. Bernard," by Ann Humphries, and "Friends," by Twyman Towery, are from *Dog Tales for the Heart,* edited by Sue A. Hershkowitz, CSP. © 1995. Published by High Impact Publications.

"Horses & Children," "Skiddor & Friends" and "Miracle Foal" are from *Horse Stories,* by Gayle Bunney. © 1998 by Gayle Bunney and Lone Pine Publishing. Published by Lone Pine Publishing.

"Roughhousing" is from *Golden Days,* by Arthur Vanderbilt. © 1998 by Arthur T. Vanderbilt. Published by Bantam Books.

"Robin, Calico and Chick," is from *The Animals in My Life,* by Grant Kendall. Copyright 1996 by Grant Kendall. Published by Howell Book House, a Simon & Schuster Macmillan Company.

"Inky," by Arnold Grobman, is from *Dog & Kennel,* October 1999.

"A Wag Is All It Took," by Mary McGrory, is from *The Washington Post,* January 2, 2000.

"The Only Choice," by Kim Owens, is from *Greyhound Tales,* edited by Nora Star. © 1997 by Nora Star. Published by Lost Coast Press.

"Danny" is from *Shelter Dogs,* by Peg Kehret. Copyright © 1999 by Peg Kehret. Published by Albert Whitman & Company.

"Coming Home," by David Redding, is from *A Friend Like No Other,* by H. Norman Wright. Originally published in *The Golden String,* by David Redding. Copyright 1987 by David Redding. Published by Fleming H. Revell Company.

"Ladybug" is from *It's a Jungle Out There,* by Gary Richmond. Copyright © 1996 by Harvest House Publishers. Published by Harvest House Publishers.

"Love Big Enough to Share," by Sheila M. Pardoe, is from *Reader's Digest,* July 1983.

"A Home for Gus" and "The Journey," by Crystal Ward Kent, are used by permission of the author.

"Mighty Hercules," by Barbara Bartocci, is from *Chicken Soup for the Cat & Dog Lover's Soul,* by Jack Canfield, Mark Victor Hansen, Marty Becker, D.V.M. and Carol Kline. © 1999 Barbara Bartocci.

"Belle" and "My First Horse" are from *Dancer on the Grass,* by Teresa tsimmu Martino. Copyright © 1999 by Teresa Martino. Published by NewSage Press.

(continued on page 208)

Designed by SMS Typography
Illustrations by Michelle Lester
Jacket designed by Dennis Arnold
Printed in the United States of America

Contents

GOOD TIMES TOGETHER

THE MEANING OF FORGIVENESS

GROWING PAINS

LOVE IS UNDERSTANDING

TREASURED MEMORIES

Introduction

If you were to ask me what my animals mean to me, I would have a hard time answering. They mean many things: they're my friends, my playmates, my teachers and trusted companions. But most of all, they're my family. I'm not unusual; most people who love animals feel the same way.

Animals fit right into the family. They love us, they want to be with us, they comfort us when things aren't going well, and when we're happy, so are they. (Wanna play ball?) They're also the world's best listeners. That's why we're devoting one of the books in our *LISTENING TO THE ANIMALS* series to animals as *One of the Family.*

Our first chapter, GOOD TIMES TOGETHER, celebrates the many ways animals and people simply enjoy being with each other. Gayle Bunney recalls Pokey, a lame horse with a great love for children. If you have ever played tug-of-war with your dog, you'll relive the experience when you read Arthur Vanderbilt's "Roughhousing." Arnold Grobman, determined to teach his dog Inky to fetch the paper for him, discovers that Inky has other plans. Ann Humphries, who doesn't see well, adopted a big dog to help her get around on her own and discovered he was also a blessing to her husband and sons.

In THE MEANING OF FORGIVENESS we are touched by our animals' ability to overlook our flaws and bring out the best in us. We meet Danny and Jessica, a remarkable dog and a young girl who help each other overcome their fears. David Redding, returning from military service, wonders whether his beloved dog will remember him. And Roberta Messner writes about the dog who helped her understand her father.

GROWING PAINS brings us stories of animals and people who still have a lot to learn about life. Sheila Pardoe wants to keep her dog all to herself until she faces up to the truth that her dog needs more than she can give him. Gus, a shelter dog who seemed unfit for adoption, gets one last chance to grow up. And a garter snake named Hercules turns out to be an answer to a mother's prayer.

The stories in LOVE IS UNDERSTANDING help us to see each other as we really are, instead of the way we appear to be. Belle, an abused horse, looks at the world with hatred until a sensitive trainer finds a way to win her trust. Reldon Bray is almost at his wits' end trying to win over a prized herding dog until he realizes that he and the dog share a common grief. Roger Caras insists that some animals have a sense of humor, and to prove his point he introduces us to Biddie, one of his favorite dogs, who knows how to laugh at herself.

TREASURED MEMORIES recalls the animals we have known, loved and sometimes lost. James Nelson writes about Ol' Spud, the dog who shared his boyhood and brought a family closer together. In "My First Horse," Teresa tsimmu Martino remembers Babe, her father's gift to her, who became her friend and inspiration. Marion Bond West shares her grief over the loss of her Collie, and the healing gift of God's comfort. In

"The Journey," Crystal Ward Kent sums it all up: What it means to love an animal.

All of the stories in *LISTENING TO THE ANIMALS* are true. They tell us about the unique bond between people and the animals who share their lives. In *One of the Family* you will meet some unforgettable friends who will make you feel right at home.

PHYLLIS HOBE

ONE OF
THE FAMILY

GOOD TIMES TOGETHER

"Some of our greatest historical and artistic treasures we place in museums... others we take for walks."

ROGER CARAS

Animals have a way of turning their time with us into memorable events. They make camping more adventurous and transform a backyard ballgame into a tournament. A walk down the street becomes a social event, and a ride in the car is like a trip around the world. Even sitting in your favorite chair with a book in your hand and your pet alongside you is happiness.

The very presence of an animal makes routine chores pleasant. Try folding your laundry while your cat makes a game of it. Or planting bulbs while your dog tries to help you by digging up the shrub bed. Laughter is only one of the rewards. It's that warm feeling in your heart that's priceless.

The Pleasure of Her Company

CAROL KNAPP

We never did learn where the friendly young Border collie came from. Unwanted animals were often abandoned in the woods outside the Spokane, Washington, city limits, but this dog looked well cared for. She appeared one morning sitting on the welcome mat on the front step of the house where I was living shortly before Terry and I were married. The grandparently friends I was living with found her, a bouncy black shadow with golden paws and a pair of golden brows above hopeful brown eyes. She was barking politely to ask if she might stay.

My friends decided that every bride and groom ought to begin life with a dog, and so it was that on an autumn afternoon a week after our wedding, Terry and I brought Bridget home to live with us. We estimated her age at six months, still a pup; and at nineteen and twenty, so were we. I had a world of growing up ahead of me, and though I didn't know it then, this wriggly black dog was going to help lead the way.

From the beginning, Bridget seemed eager to please, giving and receiving affection freely. Whenever we returned to the house, she greeted us with a hastily scavenged "welcome home" present in her mouth. It might be a stick or a sock, a scrap of paper, or even a blade of grass. I thought her gifts were wonderful until the day I bent to pet her and saw a mouse tail dangling between her teeth. I yelped and streaked for the front door, leaving one mixed-up dog to puzzle over where she had gone wrong!

In the summer, Terry and I moved from Washington to Oregon. Bridget and I became inseparable. I relied on her steady presence in my life much the same as I expected the sun to rise every day. We skittered through oak leaves on crisp autumn days kicking at acorns. At the ocean we dashed madly across the wet sand chasing after seagulls. On mountain trails she bounded ahead of Terry and me and then doubled back to make sure we hadn't lost our way. But the highlight of our escapades came in the city playground when Bridget, completely untutored, climbed the rungs of the slide at my heels and clicked her way down the slippery chute after me. I knew then I had a friend who would follow me anywhere.

The second summer of our marriage Terry and I vacationed in the Sawtooth Mountains of southern Idaho. I spotted a bear trap as we pulled into the campground, so that evening we locked our food in the car before crawling into our sleeping bags. Bridget's low growl woke us in the night. She was pacing along the inside wall of the tent keeping herself between us and the bear circling outside. Terry and I sat rooted to our pillows like a couple of stumps straight out of a petrified forest. I can still hear that bear only inches away from the tent flap slurping Bridget's soggy dog food. We had forgotten to lock her dish in the car.

Bridget didn't know it, but she was downwind of change. I was five months pregnant. Our freewheeling days together spun into memory as four babies were born in as many years. Bridget's patience outdistanced my own. She endured squalling infants, suffered toddlers sampling her food and yanking her tail, and attempted to evade kindergarteners stalking her with squirt guns. It was the cap pistol craze that began turning Bridget gray.

The years stacked up—a dozen of them. The gold in Bridget's brows began to fade. Cataracts smudged her alert brown eyes. Her rising up and settling down took longer. I was too preoccupied with my growing family to really notice these subtle changes, or maybe I didn't want to see them. Hadn't I discovered a few strands of gray in my own hair recently? Weren't Terry's eyes crinkling in new laugh lines? Time was a silent intruder.

Bridget wasn't the kind of dog who called attention to her ailments. In fact, during her twelfth summer she campaigned to prove she was as fit as ever. She caught her first ground squirrel after a lifetime of fruitless burrowing. At the lake she paddled vigorously after me when she thought I had strayed too far from shore.

Bridget's invincible spirit proved itself again in the park the next spring. At thirteen she still loved delighting children with her slide routine. But this time her agility failed her. As she reached the top of the ladder she slipped and fell backwards, slamming into the ground full on her back. She yipped once and staggered to her feet, dazed. I never asked her to climb another slide.

We left Spokane in July of that year, Terry and I and Bridget heading down the road like the old days. Only this trip there were four kids jabbering in the back seat, and the road ended in Alaska.

Bridget loved living at Big Lake. She and I sauntered through the woods on pleasant summer days. We basked in the morning sun listening to loons call. In the winter we trekked across miles of frozen lake gulping the pure air. And it was Bridget who sprawled with me on the bank of Sheep Creek one day early in the spring while I welcomed the pale filigree of leafing willows.

She had grown accustomed to these interludes when I sat quietly and acknowledged Jesus Christ as Lord, often with a Bible open in my lap. I wondered if she could sense that, in the frayed leather Book, I had found life and strength and comfort and joy. I was certain of one thing—for a dog she seemed to know a great deal.

This particular day Bridget stumbled in the twisted roots at the bank's edge and pitched into the swollen creek. I scrambled onto a log, reaching out desperately for her collar as the current carried her past me. It was a narrow escape—a close call for a shivering old dog whose sight and hearing were rapidly deserting her.

Bridget's fighting instinct remained plenty sound, however. At fourteen she was still defending us from bears. Her frenzied barking one evening alerted us to a black bear snooping around the garbage can. Terry intercepted her in mid-stride as she advanced toward the bear, who outsized her by at least three to one.

Bridget was stouthearted all right, but in spite of what she and I might believe after fourteen good years, she was not going to last forever. Now I was the one downwind of change.

She began to sleep more, to wander outdoors less. She was easily confused, barking at everything. When I had her heavy coat clipped in the spring, I saw how spindly she had become beneath the dark fur. But the bleakest loss of all came the day I called her for a walk and she stayed behind instead, wagging her tail in apology, watching me walk away. Our country jaunts were over.

Terry and I and Bridget marked fifteen years together in the autumn. At Christmas she suffered a slight dizzy spell. Then on a below-zero night in January she trudged after me to the school playground. I was ecstatic. She hadn't joined me in a walk for months. We even jogged around the bus loop kicking through knee-deep snow. What that spurt of energy must have cost her! After all her years of faithful serving I failed to recognize that Bridget was summoning her last reserve to give me a final crystal memory. She was saying good-bye.

A few days later she was unable to stand. I drove her to the veterinarian expecting him to make her well. Instead he mouthed such unthinkable terms as "uremia" and "euthanasia."

"If she were my dog," he spoke gently, "I would put her to sleep."

But she wasn't his dog. She was mine and Terry's. Inextricably bound to our beginnings. Constant like the sunrise. Losing her meant facing fearful changes I didn't want to think about. God forgive me, I couldn't let her go.

Together we had shared aloneness, explored unknown territory, tackled new responsibilities, listened to the world sing. Now this stranger was suggesting I end it. Impossible.

I brought Bridget home, but it soon became obvious she was dying. For two nights she lay on the kitchen floor whining in pain—our dog who never complained. I dialed the veterinary hospital with leaden fingers and heard myself scheduling a euthanasia appointment. The impossible was happening.

It seemed natural, sitting with Bridget those last hours, to bring out the worn Bible she had seen me open so often. I turned in need to its words of life and strength and comfort and joy—only this time I read them aloud for her too. I could taste the tears that fell as I read the Twenty-third Psalm. "Yea, though I walk through the valley of the shadow of death, I will fear no evil: for Thou art with me" (verse 4). So many walks we had taken and now this one.

Change . . . growing older . . . letting go . . . life's cadence. I couldn't alter the rhythm, but I could learn to make peace with it. The much loved Book in my lap promised that Jesus is the same yesterday, today and forever. Surely His very constancy in my life freed me to accept change. Could anything good come from losing Bridget?

Too soon it was time to leave for her appointment. Terry gently lifted her into the car. She thumped her tail feebly, trusting us to do right by her. Terry and I stood in the snow hugging each other fiercely—partly for comfort, but mostly for our brave, wonderful dog and what had been. Now it was my turn to be a faithful friend. I "walked through the valley" with Bridget to the end, cradling her in my arms, soothing her and murmuring assurances of love as she slipped peacefully from this life.

The rest of the day passed in a kind of numbed haze. Bridget was gone, yet I tried to hold her to me. I kept sniffing my sweater sleeve, where her scent still clung.

In the evening the children happened to pull out our family photo albums. I was amazed to see Bridget in so many of the pictures. There she was hiking in the mountains . . . playing at the beach . . . lying beside the Christmas tree. And she was happy. In each picture she radiated her pleasure in being with us. She knew she was loved. We had given her a good life for as long as she was in our keeping.

That's it, I thought, the key to accepting the inevitable pain of letting go. If I give my best now—loving honestly and completely, serving without holding back, savoring each phase of life—then I can rest knowing I have given the choicest portion of myself. I can let go a little easier with the certainty that I have given a good life to those who were in my keeping.

Bridget had gone. I couldn't change that. But the terrible aching inside had eased. In its place was newly won maturity. Bridget was still leading the way. On impulse I reached for my Bible and printed her name on the family memorial page. She belonged there.

The St. Bernard

ANN HUMPHRIES

$\mathcal{M}$y eyesight is severely diminished. I have retinitis pigmentosa in which I gradually lose my peripheral vision. Three years ago I stopped driving when I hit a building that I didn't see. (Hey, but guess what, *I don't have to drive*!!!) I use a cane in unfamiliar settings and in crowds, mostly to indicate to other people I don't see well. In familiar settings, I manage quite well thank-you-very-much. That's why I can walk all over the neighborhood and in the surrounding countryside without a cane. I know the territory. But, I do feel somewhat vulnerable and I must work hard at seeing which is how Noah came to live with us.

I may need a seeing eye dog in the future, but I've never had a dog of my own, only family dogs, so I was interested in being around a dog *before* I needed one. Although I claimed the dog was for our two young sons, I knew this dog would be for me.

We found Noah, our St. Bernard mix, black and white nine-month-old, 60 lb. pup at the animal shelter. He was on his back, neck on the ground, front legs folded, back legs spread, lying very, very still, tired from being held by everyone who thought he was so cute, but who didn't want a big hairy dog in their home in the South in the summer.

The eyes of the volunteers brightened when we told her what kind of dog we were looking for. Then, we saw him, lying there. Anybody will tell you to select a dog with personality and curiosity. Noah just lay there. We gathered him up, placed him in our collective laps and stroked him. Noah's legs dangled as my younger son picked him up and hugged Noah's chest to his. We walked around to inspect the other dogs and cats there. But Noah was the one. The manager/volunteer told us those dogs are frequently returned to the shelter in June and July. She tried hard to talk us out of taking him, concerned we, too, would return him. I knew he was right for us.

My husband was out of town when we brought Noah home. I had told him before he left that we may have a dog when he returned. He protested, but it was three to one. As the boys played with him in the front yard, I left a message, "Kirk, you're a daddy again." He called back and asked what kind of dog it was and I told him. "*St. Bernard*!!!!!" he shouted. I pulled the phone away from my ear and calmly said, "We don't know for sure." Of course, the boys were telling everyone they could, "Our dog is half St. Bernard," and I was shushing them as fast as I could.

That was six months ago, and yes, he's hot, he slobbers, and he's big, but he sees, hears, loves and fills a gap we didn't know we had. He, like my cane, brings out the best in people. We'll keep him!

from DOG TALES FOR THE HEART

Horses & Children

GAYLE BUNNEY

When I was a kid, my first horse wasn't exactly a saint. I suppose you could say he never actually set out to do me harm. But Patches didn't really like children, or adults for that matter either. Number one, by the time he let me catch him to go riding it was often too late in the evening to have much of a ride. He never really ran away with me, unless you count the couple of dozen times he decided to gallop home, even though I didn't want to go home yet. He never was much of a bucker unless you count the times he dumped me in the dirt, once knocking me unconscious for over an hour. He never really kicked me much or was it that I learned pretty quick to get out of the way of his heels? I wonder why it is that I don't have any great memories of Patches.

Take Pokey for instance. She was halter broke only. She was used as a brood mare only, for the simple reason that her neck was severely damaged, if not broken, when she was young. Her owner before me was a proud Granddad who when approached by his two little grandsons with the request to halter break a colt all by themselves, had said sure, go for it. They had gone down to the corrals and closed the gate on the several mares and colts standing in the shade of the barn. All those colts were pretty skittish and didn't let the two aspiring young cowboys anywhere near them. Except for a four-month-old bay filly. She stood right there and let them put a halter and lead rope on her. She even let them shoo her over next to the snubbing post. She stood watching them with big eyes as they knelt down and tied the end of the rope to the very bottom of the post, instead of whither height where it should have been tied. She was just too quiet for the youngsters, because when Granddad halter broke a horse it always fought like the dickens. So they took their midget-size cowboy hats off and spooked that filly. Terrified at the waving hats, she made one frantic lunge towards her momma over in the corner. The downward pull from the too-low tied rope was her undoing. When she hit the end of the rope, her vertebrae, up high in her neck, snapped. She toppled to the ground and lay there, unmoving, eyes begging for help. The boys knew something wasn't right when she wouldn't get up and ran to get their Granddad. He came, surveyed the damage, took the halter off her and left her there while he took the boys home to their momma's place, for he did not want to shoot an animal in front of the crying children. When he came back later with the rifle, she had got up and was hiding behind her dam. Seeing how she had got up by herself he thought just maybe she would be all right.

I bought her two months later because I felt sorry for her. She was able to graze by spreading her front legs or partially kneeling. She was unable to turn her head and neck to the right side, and the spinal column was jutted out on the right side beneath the skin. I don't have a clue as to why I bought her. I surely could not make her better, so why was I paying hard-earned money for this cripple?

She was not in pain and thrived on the extra feed and attention I gave her. She went on to raise many fine colts over the years. And if any horse loved children ever, it was Pokey. She knew not what such small humans had done to her, and she loved them.

A child to her, the smaller the better, was to be treated as one of her own children. Looking over the fence and seeing a child approaching she never failed to nicker at them, calling out to them, the same way she called to her own colts. When they were within reach, she would gently nuzzle them with her soft nose. Pokey would get upset if dogs came near any small child in her area. She would lay her ears back at a dog who bounded up to one of her human babies. I remember one time when Angie's four-year-old boy, Danny, was crying out in the corral because I said he couldn't ride Pokey anymore and had to come to the house for supper. His pitiful wails broke poor Pokey's heart. I think she was positive that her human baby was starving to death, for she kept turning her flank to him, offering her own brand of supper. Her fine muzzle caressed his hair and she talked to him with soft whinnies of love, just like she did with her own young.

Even though with her neck I had never broke her to ride, any child was more than welcome on her broad back. She would lead quietly beside me, careful to not disturb her precious cargo. Older children could sit on her all day without me anywhere near and she never attempted to get rid of them. Instead she would move extra slow and gentle as she grazed my lawn. Only God knows what a special bond he created the day he put Pokey and children together.

from HORSE STORIES

Roughhousing

ARTHUR VANDERBILT

---

*R*emember the summer storms? We always knew they were brewing if the wind was blowing up the leaves of the poplars along the shore when we took our morning walks. I know, you knew because dogs just know those things in their own ways.

Remember how all day it would feel like a storm was coming in? And the small craft warning flag would be flying at the lighthouse?

It's dusk now. The sky and Bay are timber wolf gray. Packs of waves with livid whitecap fangs race and leap down the channel, snapping and biting at Dogfish Bar and trying to tear loose from its mooring our frightened catboat. These waves mean business. We've been caught out in them before and know they want to kill. As I look up from my book out the picture window in the sunroom, I think of the director of the sailing camp down the Bay, who had sailed these waters for for years; he was out in his Sailfish when waves like these picked up. It was several days before his body was found on the backside of one of the islands. No, better be snug inside when a nor'easter howls in from the sea.

On the wall of the sunroom, the wind indicator light glowers orange, flashing north, northeast, north, northeast, east, northeast. Now rain lunges at the picture window, pounces on the roof, growls through the gutters.

"Someone take Amy out," my mother calls from the kitchen. "She hasn't been out since this morning."

My father is in the den with the game on. I look over at Marjorie, curled up asleep on the loveseat. Amy is luxuriously stretched out on the carpet, dozing and listening to the storm.

It's my turn, I know, but it's worth a try anyhow.

"Your mother wants someone to take the dog out," I say to Marjorie.

"It's your turn," she mumbles from somewhere far away, her eyes closed shut.

It is, so I don't press the issue.

"Okay, Amy, it's us," I say, reluctantly laying down *The Widow's Walk* and getting out of that particularly comfortable old Victorian rocker, the one that had been in my great grandmother's apartment, the upholstered one with the big springs under the wooden rockers. Just thinking of going out in the storm I can feel the claws of rain scratching at the back of my neck. "We're going to brave this gale and go out there and do our business, right Amy?"

Amy doesn't budge. Having learned from the master, she closes her eyes, just like Marjorie, and feigns deep sleep.

"Okay, Amy, here we go!" I say, trying to make it sound like an adventure.

For a water dog who will splash into the Bay any time, any season, Amy abhors a sprinkle of rain on her head. To even think of going out in a nor'easter clearly is out of the question. She's nestled in for the duration.

"What? Are you like some big old house cat, afraid to

get wet?" I ask in utter amazement. "A big old Maine coon pussy cat?"

A cheap trick, but that catches her attention. Without too much enthusiasm, she raises up just enough to look toward the picture window to see if there really is—and she does have serious doubts about this—a cat dumb enough to be outside in the pouring rain.

Let's get this done, whatever it takes, I think to myself, anxious to go out, come in, dry off and get back to my mystery. Maybe it's time for an old-fashioned cat scare.

I rush up to the window and look out at the storm.

"It *is* a *cat!*" I call to Amy with concern. "*A big cat!*"

From drowsy slumber to red alert in an instant, she's up and at the window, looking. *Where? Where?*

Cat scares are getting a bit old, but just often enough there actually is a suspicious-looking cat out there, lurking across the lawn stalking the quail. So it is essential for us to check out each alarm. We race from the sunroom through the living room, picking up speed as we pass through the kitchen with Amy's toenails skating over the floor. In the breezeway I grab an umbrella, and we're out on the patio, Amy at attention, looking here and there in the deluge for a sight of the evil, soggy feline intruder.

"There. I saw it there!" I say, pointing out to the bluff with my umbrella held against the wind blowing the rain straight in at the house.

The sounds of wind whipping through the pines on the bluff and waves tearing down the channel and rain lashing against the house mix in a menacing howl.

"Hurry," I urge Amy, "hurry!"

Amy senses she might have been tricked but, as not to lose face, trots out to the top of the bluff, gives a perfunctory look around for trouble, and then, finding none and knowing I'm watching intently, at least goes through a pantomime of doing what she's supposed to do (a pantomime I'm convinced on occasion she performs to get those who are obsessively concerned with her bodily functions off her back). Then, her ears blowing about like wind socks, lickety-split, she tears back to the shelter of the house.

I lock the door behind us against the storm.

In the breezeway she gives a good, deliberate head to tail shake, spraying off the rain. And that is that. She heads back to the sunroom, dark now but for the light from the table lamp by my rocker, and resumes her nap that was so rudely interrupted.

"Did you dry her with a towel?" my mother calls from the kitchen a few minutes after I'm settled in the rocker and am back into my Nantucket murder mystery.

"What?"

"Did you dry the dog with a towel?" . . .

"Make sure her chest is dry," my mother reminds me as I walk out to the back hall to get from the bottom of the closet the old orange bath towel. "The chest is the most important part to get bone dry."

Now, since the time when man first invited dog to come live in his house, there has always been a lot of give and take in making this cross-species relationship work. At times, the relationship can be so close that we believe dogs are very much like us, that we, indeed, are related, that we're parents or children, brothers or sisters. And dogs, studies have shown, watch us and know us better than we know them. Maybe dogs find that we become more like them, and maybe we do. They adopt us into their packs as we adopt them into our families. Yet there will always be things about dogs we just cannot comprehend, like what it is that is so ecstatically delightful in sliding into something dead and smelly and squishing it up real tight behind the ears, just as there must be many things about us that dogs cannot fathom, like the endless idle hours we spend seated before the flickering images in a big black box.

With few exceptions, what Amy might not fully understand, she gamely accepts. And one of those few exceptions is getting toweled dry. For the supreme leader of a pack to be dried off behind the ears and have her tummy rubbed dry after being outside in the rain is, to her, completely incomprehensible and unreasonable. Clearly it is unacceptable.

Carrying the orange bath towel into the sunroom is like pirouetting with a red cape through the streets of Pamplona during the running of the bulls. As soon as Amy sees it coming, she charges it, grabbing hold of a corner, and, hanging on, shakes it like a partridge.

She has her end, I have mine, with which I quickly go to work.

"Oh, nice and dry, we're going to get you so nice and dry," I singsong chant, toweling under each ear and around her throat. "Ohhhhh, so beautiful, such beautiful, lovely, luscious golden hair, so soft and silky, golden blond, honey blond, lustrous honey blond hair, uummm, so smooth and soft."

Nodding slowly in agreement, she momentarily succumbs to this soothing beautyshop lullaby, almost letting her end of the towel drop from her mouth.

She catches herself just as it does, and grabs it with a snap.

"Amy get dry," I patiently explain, prying open her jaws and pulling out the gooey end, only to have her lunge for another hunk of it.

She looks up at me to see how I'm taking it.

"Now wait a minute," I indignantly protest. "Wait just a minute! They wouldn't put up with this in a beauty parlor, and you know it."

With her hanging on to one end of the towel, all the while slyly waiting to reel in more if I relax my hold on it, I work with the few square inches of towel she's left me, drying around the ears, under the chin, down the chest, the back, the tail, the legs, rolling her over on her back to get the stomach. Swishing her tail back and forth, her black lips grinning, she grabs more towel, which she holds in her jaws and flails with her paws.

"This is so silly, Amy. Why would a dog even think of something like this? What would a dog? What would a dog even be thinking?" I ask Amy in astonishment as she rolls back over on her stomach, tugging at her end of the towel and staring right at me, defiantly.

"What's she doing?" Marjorie asks, wide awake now that all the dirty work has been done and the fun might be beginning.

"I think she's being defiant. To me, at least," I say, tugging at my end of the towel to get more back, "this smacks of defiance. Do we have to take it?"

"No we do not," Marjorie states emphatically, descending from the loveseat to the carpet to the scene of impending battle. "Give me that end."

And the games begin.

"Is she dry?" my mother calls in, not fully appreciating the enormity of the task she has assigned. To her, Amy always is a little girl who can be dressed up in ribbons and ruffles for tea parties, a sweet little girl all sugar and spice and everything nice.

"Yup. As dry as she's going to get," I answer.

"Did you get the chest? The chest is most important."

"It's as dry as I can get it."

I neglect to report that our beauty parlor patron is currently engaged in a rousing game of tug-of-war, with Marjorie manning the other end of the orange towel.

Already the game is getting pretty intense.

"Amy, you're a brute and you know it," Marjorie says.

All golden retrievers like to fantasize that they can be fierce, and Amy redoubles her tugging.

"Come on, one hand," I tell my sister. "Give her a chance."

"Give her a chance? Give her a chance?" she hisses at me, hanging on to the towel for dear life. "This is not a retriever you brought back in. This is some kind of wolf dog that's loose in the house."

And sure enough, Amy's lovely and loving brown eyes have assumed the frightening steely glint of the Big Bad Wolf's eyes in that split second when Little Red Riding Hood suddenly perceived that it was not Grandmama under the covers.

"One hand, one hand, those are the rules," I remind her again. "She's only got one mouth."

"Okay, okay," my sister mutters, letting go with one hand and instantly losing several inches of towel as Amy pulls back against the momentary slack.

"I told you! She's not playing fair."

"She's playing fair, and she's going to beat you if you don't watch out."

Now the match gets serious, and a gambling man in that dark room with the wind wailing about the eaves would have had a hard time knowing where to place his bet: on a Wellesley graduate sprawled on the floor, one end of a towel clenched in her hand, pulling for all she was worth, or on a wily retriever with the other end of the towel clenched in bared teeth, her eyes becoming more and more demonic, a low warning rumbling from her throat, watching, watching, waiting for that split second of weakness, a moment of exhaustion, a repositioning.

Now!

In a movement almost too quick to see, Amy lets go of the towel and pounces on it several inches closer to the middle, an ominous growl in her throat defying anyone to call that cheating; and is that a look of triumph in her eyes?

"See! I told you! That's cheating!" my sister declares.

Bully on you, Amy seems to reply as she repeats her tactic and lunges again at the towel, grabbing it inches from my sister's fingers.

Marjorie lets go as if she touched a mouse crouched in the dusty dark corner of a cupboard and jumps back out of the way.

"Good gods, Amy, you win. Okay? I quit. You win. You can have the stupid towel. It's yours."

Amy already knows she has won without waiting for that gracious concession speech. She grabs my sister's end of the towel, lying over the rest of it, and begins a methodical ripping, viciously shaking a hunk.

Game over, right? Amy has won fair and square, everyone is ready to concede that. But woe be unto whoever tries to retrieve that towel. This is the really hard part of the game.

Left to her devices, Amy will make a great show of angrily ripping loose every thread of the hated towel, mash around a bunch until they're nice and soggy, and then swallow, which isn't good for the drying towel or for a golden retriever. Our mission impossible is to take the towel away and let it dry out for another rainy day.

"Here, get the towel," I breezily tell my sister as if it's the simplest matter in the world.

"Are you crazy? I'm not going near it," she says from the safety of the loveseat, her bare feet tucked under her. "You get it."

Amy is waiting for just such an eventuality, her eyes challenging anyone who comes within five feet of her. Any closer and she lets go of the towel and assumes her protective position, huddling over it, trying to get a more threatening look in her eye, closer still and a warning snarl, then a wrinkling of the nose, a show of fierce retriever teeth, the hair on the back of her neck magically rises, and if anyone is foolish enough to lay even a finger on a stray corner of that towel, Attack! the most ferocious, fiercest, most bloodcurdling snarl and lunge at those misplaced fingers as if she meant to tear them out at the roots.

Amy never actually connects with human flesh, perhaps because she doesn't really intend to and is merely training us to be fair. Or perhaps she is just having some fun bullying us (she always seems to chuckle to herself as soon as she snarls and, like the gracious winner of a heated tennis match, trots right over to shake hands). Or maybe under these circumstances of imminent peril, misplaced human fingers can retreat pretty quickly. But her response always is the same. And, upon reflection, it does make sense: she has won the game, fair and square. The trophy is hers. That is retriever fairness. And who could argue with that?

But still there is the matter of getting the towel back while it still resembles a towel and not merely its constituent threads. As Mr. Darling in *Peter Pan* learned with Nana, all the sweet talk in the world will get you nowhere. Fair, after all, is fair. To the victor belong the spoils.

It's time to play our trump card: cheese.

Like old Ben Gunn marooned on Treasure Island, Amy dreams of cheese, long, sweet, deliciously repetitive dreams of cheese. For a good morsel of cheese, there isn't anything she won't do.

We know it will work.

"Would you like a little piece of cheese?" we ask as she glares at us, awaiting our next move.

She looks at us, suspiciously, considering our offer, still holding the towel firmly in clenched jaws, not about to be fooled by the old Trojan Horse ploy.

"No, really. A little bit of *cheese*?"

It always helps to describe exactly what kind of cheese we're talking about.

"We've got some of that new sharp Cheddar *cheese.* Yup, the strong kind. From Vermont. It's pretty good *cheese.*"

The towel is dropped, long forgotten, the last thing on her mind. Who wants a dry, tasteless towel when there's cheese being distributed?

She's up. She's herding us toward the kitchen six inches from our legs, faster, faster. *Must get that cheese.*

Into the bright kitchen she skips, as sweet and innocent as little Miss Muffet, her wolf mask put away. Straight to the refrigerator where fabulous stashes of cheese are stored. Out comes the slab of golden cheese from the back of the refrigerator door. It is laid on the counter. Two brown eyes watch in salivating anticipation, like Ben Gunn's, as it is placed on a breadboard, the wrapper opened, a paring knife taken from a drawer, a nice hunk neatly cut from it and, like a pirate's gold bar, divided into thirds.

"What's that for?" my mother asks.

"We had to promise her cheese to get the towel back," my sister explains.

"Oh, don't be ridiculous," my mother responds. "She always

lets me dry her, don't you, Amy? Amy, you have them buffaloed, that's what I think."

A tasty morsel of strong Vermont Cheddar cheese, down the hatch in a gulp. And a healthy half of the other two pieces from the tug-of-war losers.

Pots bubble and simmer on the stove. The smell of chicken roasting in the oven catches Amy's interest. She looks up at my mother, expectantly, as if to ask, *Is there anything I can do to help in the kitchen? Is it ready yet? Can I have a piece now?* Amy knows by heart the answers to each of these kitchen questions, but her philosophy is that it never hurts to ask. And she knows, too, that at dinnertime, merely by resting her head in our laps and poking her nose into the stomachs of those pack members she can so easily dominate, she will secure all the chicken she wants, no hunting or skinning required.

Our work is done. We're in for the night, cozy and warm. The orange towel is out of sight, having been secreted in the washing machine. Everyone is content. We three head back to the sunroom to resume our dozing and sleeping and reading, as outside the wind drives sheets of rain against the house as if the storm will blow all night.

from GOLDEN DAYS

Robin, Calico and Chick

GRANT KENDALL

This is sort of a flashback.

From the time I was three until I was six, my parents owned a seven-acre "farm," where we kept a couple of horses and various other forms of animal life.

A dog was always present, and at the time we are discussing the resident canine was a black Cocker Spaniel named Robin. There were at least three cats (maybe more; I recall only three). They were all supposed to be barn cats, but I was extremely fond of one, a calico that we had cleverly named Calico. Calico's function as a barn cat was severely compromised by me; I would carry her to the house nearly every day.

One day at the beginning of my six-year-old summer, I was told we were moving. We had sold the seven-acre place and were moving to a ten-acre spread only six miles away. It was even on the same road.

The horses were trailered over. Robin rode over with us in the car.

"When will we bring the cats?" I asked.

"They're not coming," my mother said.

"But they're our cats," I protested.

"We'll get new cats."

"But who will take care of them?"

"We told the people who bought the place that they were there. They were glad to hear it; they said they needed barn cats. They'll take good care of them," Mom explained.

This wasn't particularly well received by me, but six-year-olds rarely have a vote in family matters. I didn't understand this at the time, but since then I have had children of my own, each of whom was six at one time, and now I more fully appreciate my parents' thinking.

The new place had a nicer barn and more paddocks. It also had a creek running through it that abounded in fish (mostly perch and minnows). There were little pools where tadpoles teemed, and it also contained some of nature's most amazing— to a six-year-old—creatures: crawdads.

Overall, this was a good place. But I wanted a cat.

We had been there maybe three weeks and I had asked about acquiring a cat almost daily.

"Wait until we're settled," was the stock answer.

There *was* some confusion, that was sure. A lot of stuff was still in boxes. Looking back now, I see the problem: We'd gone from a house that had a living room, four bedrooms and a den to a house that had a living room, four bedrooms and *no* den. I think the new place was larger, square-foot-wise, but there was a roomful of furniture and other accoutrements that had to be fitted in somewhere.

While in this state of confusion, the farm itself was pretty much ignored. The horses were fed and watered, but that was about it. I was told that the matter of a cat would be attended to in time.

But one morning, after we had been there about three weeks, I got up at my usual time—six or six-thirty—to go outside and play. "Play" consisted of Robin and me going down to the creek to count tadpoles and marvel at crawdads, or just generally to investigate. No one else was ever up when we set off on our treks.

This particular morning, as I stepped out the back door of the kitchen, a cat ran up to me, meowing frantically. It was Calico!

Over the centuries many stories have been written and told about animals that were lost or left behind and that traversed vast distances and finally were reunited with their loved ones. At the age of six I hadn't heard any of them, but since then I believe them all. Calico had only come six miles, and I assume it had taken her three weeks to do it (of course, she may have only started out the night before, for all I knew), but she did it.

I immediately took her in to see my parents and my big brother, all of whom were thrilled to see her at six-thirty in the morning. My brother, who probably wouldn't have gotten up until noon otherwise, was especially overjoyed.

"*Mom!* Get this brat outta here before I break his neck!" I think is how he expressed his delight.

Calico settled in. She joined Robin and me on our expeditions.

There was a very shallow area in the creek where I could walk across and not even get the tops of my feet wet. Robin, of course, splashed through with glee, but the first time Calico went there with us she stayed back, not caring to risk the dangers of the water. She sat there waiting, and when we returned she continued on our rounds with us.

The next time we ventured across the creek, which was probably the next morning, Calico sat quietly until Robin and I had gotten to the other side. I looked back and said, "We'll be back, Calico. Stay there." At which point she leaped into the shallow water!

She got her feet under her, then picked a front paw up out of the water and shook it. She put it back down, picked up the other one and shook it, too, then repeated the action with each hind foot. Then she leaped another foot or two and repeated the paw shaking. The creek was probably only six feet wide at this point, so in a couple more bounds she was out on the other side with us. After each forward move, though, she would pick up her paws, one at a time, shake them, then put them back down in the water.

After we finished whatever it is little boys and animals do, we crossed back over the creek, Calico returning in the same manner. But in time she learned that if she walked gingerly instead of leaping, she would splash less, thereby not completely soaking herself. She always shook her paws off after each step, though.

Later that summer there was a fair in the area. I don't know if it was state or county or something totally different, but we all went. It was necessary for me to play all the games they offered, of course; I believe they each cost a dime then. I never won anything; my brother told me no one ever did, and he knew everything. After all, he was fourteen and had been around.

One of the games consisted of what appeared to be a jillion soft drink bottles all pushed up next to each other. For ten cents, participants got to toss three Ping-Pong balls, and if one—only one!—landed atop a bottle, the tosser was a winner.

I watched several people try. My brother and his friend Sonny both tried. The balls bounced on and across the bottles, never even trying to stop. I told Mom I wanted to try. She gave me a dime.

First toss: I missed the bottles entirely. My Ping-Pong ball went straight to the ground.

Second toss: It bounced on and over, the same as the others I had seen.

Third toss: Miracles do still occur! Or at least they did back then. The ball bounced up and around and back and forth and finally came to rest atop a bottle! I won!

Then came the question of what I had won.

The prize turned out to be a baby chick! What a neat prize!

"It'll die," my brother proclaimed.

"Hush, Alan," our mother said. "Honey, you don't really want a chicken, do you?"

"Yes!"

"It'll die," the voice of doom persisted.

"You're just jealous!" I informed him.

We took the chick, which I had named Chick, home and made him a residence in a box in the garage. We placed some water in a mayonnaise jar lid, and my brother got a handful of horse feed, crushed it with a hammer and tossed it in the box with Chick.

Despite the fatal prophecy, Chick lived and thrived and grew—if horses grew as rapidly, they could race as weanlings—and eventually he turned into a rooster. I imagine he had been a rooster all along, but the discovery was exciting nonetheless.

Robin and Calico had discovered Chick early. They showed only mild interest, so when Chick attained the size—and bowel habits—too big for the garage, we had only minimal fear of turning him out in the world.

We carried him outside and put him down in the middle of the backyard. Robin and Calico eyed him with interest but took no action.

We left him out for three or four hours that first day, then put him back in the garage for the night. The next day he would be put out early and left, I was informed.

So the next morning I took him back outside.

Robin and Calico and I left him in the yard and made our rounds. When we returned, Robin spotted Chick from about sixty or seventy feet away and took off toward him, barking ferociously!

Chick, seeing and hearing what must have appeared to be the Hound of Hell, took off as fast as he could, flapping and squawking and making general frantic chicken sounds.

Calico, aware that something was afoot, took off, too, yowling and hissing.

I panicked! I ran toward the house, crying and screaming. Robin was gaining rapidly on Chick, and Calico was right behind him.

Before I could get to the house to rouse some help, Robin caught Chick, jumped on him, and Calico joined in!

There were cat howls and dog growls and chicken squawks. Fur and feathers were flying. And I was sobbing and screaming for them to stop.

And then they did. All three lay there for a moment, panting, and then got up and shook themselves off. I ran over to them and rolled them over and examined them, but, except for a small patch of hair and a feather or two, nobody was hurt.

After a few minutes, Chick got up and crowed and flapped his wings and started running. Calico leaped to her feet instantly. She was after him! Robin began barking and took off, too.

So here's the picture: a rooster running full speed, flapping his wings and making wild chicken sounds, followed by a cat, also at top speed, yowling, followed by a dog, going full out and barking maniacally.

Calico caught Chick just as Robin caught them both. Again, fur and feathers flew from the cloud of dust and din.

And, again, it all stopped and all three combatants lay there gasping. And, again also, all three were unharmed.

They took considerably longer to regroup this time. I went to the house to get Mom, who would probably be up by now. It was after seven.

"Mom, come and see!" I yelled to her.

She came out to the yard just as Chick got up and crowed and flapped. Then he took off, and the whole frantic scene was repeated.

Mom took off after them as I tried to stop her. A six-year-old is no match for a relatively fit thirty-six-year-old, however, and she soon outdistanced me, shouting for Robin to stop, which he did, just as soon as all three crashed into a snarling, growling, squawking heap.

This went on all day. They must have done it fifteen times, and none of them was ever hurt.

That evening I wanted to bring Chick into the garage but was voted down. Mom told Alan to help me take him to the barn. We left him there in a stall with a handful of horse feed.

The next morning I went out to explore with my friends, but Robin and Calico weren't there to greet me. I called for them, and Robin came out of his doghouse and came running to me. And coming out of the doghouse, right behind him, were Calico and Chick.

We investigated about an acre of woods next to the house that morning—and Chick came with us.

As we came back into the back yard, Chick began flapping and crowing and the chase was on again!

This continued several times every day from then on, and

each night the unlikely trio would sleep together in Robin's doghouse.

I had always liked animals, but I loved these three. And I think this is when the idea of becoming a veterinarian first entered my mind.

from THE ANIMALS IN MY LIFE

Friends

TWYMAN TOWERY, PhD., FACHE

The first time I saw Clyde was when he and his litter mates were tearing across the yard and he tripped and started rolling toward me like a little, round fluffy ball. Little did I know that in less than two years Clyde would be hunting the swamps and bayous of Louisiana like a seasoned professional.

A lot of bird dog men make fun of Brittanies, thinking these little critters could never match their wide ranging Setters and Pointers. Clyde, with his splash of orange and white, cropped tale and floppy ears, running through the bush, made a believer out of everyone who observed him. In Tennessee, an old friend and the best bird hunter I've ever roamed the hills with, scoffed at the very idea of a Brittany being able to match his veteran setters. But by the end of our first hunt, my hunting partner was paying attention to Clyde over the other dogs—the greatest compliment my little buddy could have received.

But Clyde's greatest trait was being a wonderful companion to both children and adults. He loved being a member of the family. People who think a dog can't be a rugged hunter and a loving friend both, don't really know dogs. The talented Clyde was dearly loved by all who experienced him.

At seven years old a cruel infection invaded Clyde and we could only watch while he suffered a slow, painful good-bye.

My vet called on a dreary Saturday afternoon and said he had taken Clyde outside for a few minutes, where he went into his hunting posture—and died. The space Clyde left in our hearts was unfillable.

The next day, I had to take an early morning flight on a business trip and found myself at the ticket counter crying. Everyone was embarrassed and looked away. Later I was sobbing in the boarding area and people changed seats to avoid me. I upgraded to first class with a frequent flyer coupon and sat alone. Once into the air the tears started flowing and the sobs ripped loose again. A flight attendant stopped, sat down by me, and asked what was wrong. I told her and she told me about her dog who had died almost two years ago. We cried together and held hands. And we both felt better.

from DOG TALES FOR THE HEART

A Blue Christmas?

STARLA "MISTY" SPRAY

Lectures. Term papers. Finals. Grades. College was nothing but pressure on top of pressure. I was carrying a full course load at Bauder in Arlington, Texas, the fall semester of my sophomore year and feeling like I had a weight the size of the Lone Star State on my shoulders. The fact that it was Friday didn't matter one bit. I was looking at a weekend of studying. I wondered where I would find time even for church on Sunday.

I drove my usual route home to my parents' and hoped the familiar sights along the way would ease my stress. But the big old weeping willow I'd watched grow from a skinny sapling, my high school alma mater, the garland-wrapped streetlights downtown—that day they didn't do a thing for me.

I turned onto North Center Street and drove by the lawn with the big plastic Nativity figures. The crib was empty, and the light in the cow had burned out. I slowed the car while some tall boys moved their football game out of the street. Up ahead was the weather-beaten two-story house that always stuck in my mind. The paint was chipped and peeling, the steps to the front porch sagged, and I imagined big empty rooms inside. The frail old man who lived there was sitting out front, as usual, his black Lab lying lazily in the tall grass at his feet. *He's got his Bible out again,* I noted. Once I'd heard him reciting passages to the dog! A couple times I'd felt the urge to stop and say hi, just talk to him for a few minutes, see if he was all right, but I was always too busy. I glanced in my rearview mirror. "Reading the Bible to a dog," I murmured, hitting the brakes. "How lonely can a person get?"

In the next open driveway I turned the car around, breaking up the boys' ball game again. I parked in front of the run-down house and got out of my car. "Hi," I called to the old man, suddenly feeling awkward. "Nice day, isn't it?"

"Come on and sit awhile," he said, scooting over on the steps to make room for me. "I'm Diggs," he said, "and that's my dog, Blue."

"Pleasure to meet you, Mr. Diggs. Everybody calls me Misty." We shook hands, and I took a seat. Up close the man didn't seem so frail. His eyes were soft and content. "I've often seen you out here reading," I said, reaching to pat Blue's head.

Mr. Diggs smiled. "Mostly I read the Bible. I have plenty of time for reading these days."

"You live alone?" I asked.

"I wouldn't put it that way exactly," Mr. Diggs said. "My wife and most of my friends are gone from this world, but I'm never alone. Not as long as I have my faith." Blue let loose an expressive whine and nosed Mr. Diggs's shoe. "Yes, yes, boy," he laughed, "and I've got you too. But that goes without saying." He leaned over to rub Blue's back, and I saw how much he loved him.

"Blue likes to listen to me read," Mr. Diggs said. "You have time for a story, Misty?"

"Maybe just one," I said, getting a little nervous about everything I had to do.

The old man turned to the story of the first Christmas in

Luke. *I hope this doesn't take too long,* I thought. Blue rested his chin on his crossed paws as if pleased to sit and listen all day. I scratched my knee and tried to sneak a peek at my watch.

"'Behold,'" Mr. Diggs read, slowing down as he repeated the angel's holy announcement, "'I bring you good tidings of great joy . . .'"

Christmas had always been a joyful time for me too, but that year it had taken a backseat to school. Everything had. I stayed quiet, though, till Mr. Diggs finished. When he had, part of me was sorry. He had a way about him that was calming, and while he was reading, his voice a little like a good preacher's, I'd almost forgotten my worries. "I'd better get going," I said. "My parents will be holding dinner, and I have loads of schoolwork."

Mr. Diggs invited me back anytime. "Old Blue and I will be here. You can count on that."

I said I'd stop by again, but pretty quick I fell back into my routine of studying, studying and more studying, and worrying about studying in between. On the day before school let out for Christmas break, I drove down North Center Street again. Mr. Diggs was there on the porch, head in his hands. Something was wrong. I stretched my neck to look into the tall grass. Blue! He was gone! No way could I stop. What would I say? I sped by. At home I threw myself onto my bed, feeling guilty.

When I refused my mom's meatloaf and mashed potatoes, she figured I had a flu bug. I knew different. I was sick of myself. It was time to get my nose out of my books and do something that wasn't about *me.*

On Christmas Eve I drove the familiar route toward school. I didn't have class; Mom had said I could invite Mr. Diggs over for Christmas dinner. I turned down North Center Street, passed the big Nativity scene and parked in front of the old house. *Why isn't he outside on a nice day like this?* I wondered, walking up to the porch. I knocked hard on the door and heard shuffling footsteps inside. Mr. Diggs pulled open the door and smiled. "Come on in, Misty," he said. "What a surprise."

I stepped inside, and when he closed the door the house fell quiet. Blue was nowhere to be seen, except in pictures scattered all around the den. There were other pictures too, of Mr. Diggs and his wife, waving from a ship, sharing a beach umbrella, sitting at a tiny table in a fancy restaurant. But mostly there were pictures of Blue. Mr. Diggs saw me staring at the one of Blue swimming with a big stick in his mouth. "He played fetch in the gulf for two solid hours that day," he remembered. "There was a bit of an undertow, but Blue was a mighty strong swimmer."

Was? I looked at Mr. Diggs.

"Blue's disappeared," he said, his voice shaky. "I can't hardly sit out on the porch these days. It makes me miss him all the more."

"I'm sorry, Mr. Diggs. Really I am. Your wife, your friends . . . now Blue." I began to cry. He'd lost everything.

Mr. Diggs handed me his hankie. "Don't forget, Misty, I've got my faith. That's the constant in my life. Hard as they may be, the rough patches pass. I've prayed for Blue to come home, and now it's up to the Lord."

I sniffled. "But what if Blue doesn't come back . . . *ever*?"

"He's in the Lord's capable hands. So am I. So are you too, Misty."

I was amazed that even now he was ready to accept whatever God had in store.

"Do you believe in Christmas?" Mr. Diggs asked. "In the

promise of Jesus' birth? God never leaves us. No matter what else may be happening in our lives, happy or sad, Christmas is coming. And Christmas *always* comes, Misty. You can count on that."

I dried my eyes. "That's why I stopped by, actually. To invite you to spend tomorrow with my family." Mr. Diggs accepted, and I raced home to tell Mom to set the extra place at our table.

When I arrived on Christmas Day to pick him up, Mr. Diggs was wearing an old gray suit and a tad too much aftershave. He offered his arm and escorted me to my car. As he held open my door I noticed something in the distance: a parade of children coming up the street. I recognized the tall boys whose football game I'd disrupted. Younger kids led the pack. A black spot next to one of the kids started to take shape as they moved toward us. Could it be?

"Blue!" Mr. Diggs shouted, and his friend came running. The kids caught up and gathered around us, telling how they'd seen the dog several blocks away and knew he belonged on North Center Street. We all petted Blue and welcomed him home. "How 'bout taking a nap till I get back?" Mr. Diggs said. Blue circled a few times, then lay down in his spot in the tall grass. The neighborhood kids promised to keep an eye on him while they played outside with their new bikes and roller skates.

Mr. Diggs waved to them as we drove down North Center Street past the lawn with the big Nativity. The baby lay in the manger, and the light in the cow had been replaced. "See what I told you, Misty?" Mr. Diggs said. "Christmas always comes."

We enjoyed our day together, and when I brought Mr. Diggs home, Blue was there waiting.

Driving to school the first day classes resumed, I saw the old man at his usual post. This time, though, Blue wasn't the sole audience for his Bible reading. At Mr. Diggs's feet were 9 or 10 kids from the neighborhood. I honked and waved. College wasn't going to get any easier, but the rough patches would pass. And after all, Christmas was only a few hundred days away.

Inky

ARNOLD GROBMAN

---

*I*nky was a puppy of uncertain parentage, who closely resembled a black-and-tan hound. A few days after he joined our household, we found a note under our door from the superintendent of the apartment house. The gist of the note was that dogs weren't allowed in the building. The message required diplomacy at the highest level, and so my wife, Hulda, met with the superintendent to see if an understanding could be reached. The summit meeting ended with these four major points of agreement:

1. We would hire the superintendent's young son, Bruce, to take Inky for a walk at noontime and every afternoon when he came home from school.

2. We would pay Bruce a dollar a week.

3. Should the apartment house owner come by, the superintendent would explain that the dog was just visiting.

4. Inky would remain with us.

The compact served well all of the parties—Inky, Hulda, Bruce, the superintendent, and me—for as long as we lived in the apartment house.

Apparently other residents in the apartment complex realized that Inky was more than a temporary visitor, for we frequently found small bags of bones at our front door that had been placed there by sympathetic neighbors.

One day a neighbor stopped by with a large package in her hand. She had been to the butcher shop and had bought a standing roast. This was during World War II, and shortages had resulted in meat being strictly rationed. Our neighbor must have spent a month's worth of red ration points for that large standing roast, but she said the meat just didn't look right to her and asked if Inky would like it.

We assured her that Inky would like it, and she left it with us. We also were quite sure that Inky would be glad to share the roast with us. Hulda, Inky and I feasted on the roast for the best part of a week—the only beef any of us had for a long, long time.

World War II ended, and we left Rochester, New York, to accept appointments at the University of Florida. Hulda, Inky and I drove to Gainesville, Florida, and found a chaotic housing situation there. Hulda and I were unable to find a place to live in Gainesville. We finally located an "apartment" in Melrose, about 20 miles east of Gainesville. The apartment was two rooms on the second floor of an old house. We obtained hot water for dish washing and cooking by heating a kettle of water on a kerosene stove on the front screened porch after carrying the water from the back-porch spigot. To dispose of the water, it was carried back from the front screened porch, through the living room, hall and bedroom, to the back screened porch, where it was poured into a large funnel that emptied into the yard.

Dogs weren't allowed in the apartment, and so we placed Inky in a kennel. The monthly charge for the kennel—for one dog—was three dollars more than the rent for our apartment—for two people. I am sure the value received accurately reflected the differential in the charges. I hope Inky realized how fortunate he was under the prevailing circumstances.

As soon as we could, we bought a house in Gainesville, and the world looked much brighter. Inky could join us and leave the kennel. Our little family was reunited.

After we were finally settled in our new Gainesville house, my normal routine was to stagger out of bed in the morning and bring the newspaper to our dining room table so we could read it during breakfast. One morning it was raining, and the thought occurred to me that it would be nice if Inky would learn to fetch the paper so that I wouldn't have to go outside in my pajamas on rainy days.

Accordingly I began the necessary training program, and in a few days, Inky understood his assignment. I would open the front door and call, "Inky, paper." He would dash out, run around the front yard until he found the rolled-up newspaper, and then bring it in. I was pleased, thinking how helpful he would be on rainy days.

A few days later it rained. That morning I called, "Inky, paper." He dashed to the door but stopped abruptly.

My original plan had been that I would pick up the paper on fair days and Inky would fetch it on rainy days. Instead, after the training period, we established the procedure that Inky would get the paper on fair days and I would fetch it on rainy days.

It was quite clear who had trained whom.

from DOG & KENNEL

A Wag Is All It Took

MARY McGRORY

$\mathcal{W}$ould you excuse me if I hang back in the old century for just a few minutes? I feel that with all the treachery going on both in technology and among humans, I would mention a few dogs I saw over the holidays who embody the loyalty, concern, goodwill toward men and other qualities that are not vastly on display elsewhere in the world.

I speak first of Harry, my cousin Brian's golden retriever, an elegant and amiable creature, with just a dash of con man and pol in his nature to give it spice. He, of course, came with his master to meet me at the airport. My cousin had kindly invited me to a holiday lunch at Boston's incomparable Ritz Cafe. The only hitch was that Brian had to shop for his entire gift list before we could sit down to scrod prepared by a band of angels. This involved my waiting outside with Harry, while Brian raced up and down the aisles grabbing gifts with a bandit's speed. The entryway to Lord & Taylor was unheated and the temperature was 25, and people scurried in, not just desperate but frozen.

Harry had a miraculous effect on them. Everyone spoke to him. The most clouded countenance lifted and broke into a smile at the sight of him. People who obviously did not have time to breathe stopped to scratch his ears and whisper endearments. They wished him a Merry Christmas, often graciously including me in the greeting.

One young woman, who seemed especially stricken by the stress of the season, came out of the store empty-handed. She sank to one knee to kiss him on the forehead. Harry, of course, responded in kind and licked her face. She thanked us both.

Others asked his name, age and sex. An older couple came toiling into view. The man asked, "Boy or girl?" I said, "His name is Harry." "We have a girl," he said. "Her name is Rosie. Would you like to see her picture?" He whipped out his wallet and proudly showed me a dog like Harry.

"She's very smart," he said. "Harry," I replied boldly, "sits down, without being told, the minute he gets to a curbstone and doesn't move until his master tells him to."

I felt we could go on indefinitely extolling our pets' champion qualities. The man's wife, pale in the jaws of the Christmas crunch, towed him away.

Harry had given us all an excuse to be nice to each other; he had brought out the best in everyone, as dogs so often do. I was chilled to the bone by the time Brian reappeared, but my heart was warm.

The next day, it was my feet.

We went to Christmas dinner at Jud and Maryann's stately new mansion. It was garlanded and festooned, and everything was what it ought to be except that I was still cold. People were very kind. They gave me a seat by the fire, a lap robe, a brandy. Happily, the household includes two blond Labradors, and one of them, Murphy, is a humanitarian. He cased the situation, then came over and lay down on my feet—not at them, on them. Instant Palm Beach was the result.

And Murphy stayed there. Samantha, the other lab, started at the sound of cars or sudden sallies by the children. Murphy the Merciful never budged. I told his mistress that it was remarkable that he had sensed a need and filled it with no fuss. "He's that way," she said with understandable pride.

Danny, who belongs to my niece Anne and her husband, Tom, is also a golden, but not yet into social work. He is young. He sits by your chair when you are eating your breakfast, and sometimes he puts his head in your lap. He beams upon you a melting gaze that would make a saint feel guilty. He is all but saying, "It's entirely up to you, but I want you to remember that if you cannot finish that cranberry bread but don't want to hurt Anne's feelings by leaving any, I am here for you. I want to help."

Coming back on the plane, I read a riveting New York Times story about a furor in England over a Yuletide television special, part of a series called "One Man and His Dog." It's about shepherds steering their sheep into pens with the indispensable help of their sheep dogs.

The English keep a tight rein on their emotions, but when it comes to dogs, they just let 'em rip. According to the Times's reporter, Sarah Lyall, the English are riled that some of their countrymen might seek more piquant TV fare. I am with the dog lovers. Marveling at dogs who cope with silly sheep is an excellent corrective for Internet heads who think they know it all.

I also hope somebody makes a documentary about a program called Therapy Dog Training that certifies some specially trained breeds—Rottweilers among them—as caseworkers in nursing homes and mental hospitals. Seems they're born shrinks. People pour out their hearts to them. I think every now and then, it's good to remember that while we train dogs, they can teach us a whole lot about love and devotion as well as just being nice.

from THE WASHINGTON POST

The Only Choice

KIM OWENS

My husband Robert and I are just crazy about our three adopted greyhounds but their adoption came about in an unusual way. Now we would not take any amount of money for our dogs, but in the beginning we had no idea that we would be changed forever. As our story unfolds, you will see that we really had only one choice to make!

It all started about two years ago with a conversation on greyhounds. We had a friend who worked at a kennel in Florida, and she would return home to our area occasionally to visit. I have been an animal lover all of my life, but I must admit that the plight of retired racers had somehow passed me by. Robert and I weren't aware of what was happening, or about the various rescue efforts happening all over the country. As our friend told us all this, I found myself petting the large greyhound with her who was already leaning heavily on my legs. Neither one of us could take our eyes off "King" who was destined for an arranged adoption. Those big golden eyes had me and I could barely tear myself away. Two minutes petting a sick dog and my life was changed forever. We hadn't thought about getting another dog for our menagerie at home, so this presented a whole new ballgame. She told us to think about it, because the choice is truly a long term one. She would be coming home again soon, and could bring us a dog. We exchanged phone numbers and I promised to call. Before she left, she gave me the wonderful book *Adopting the Racing Greyhound* by Branigan. "Read this," she said, "then call me. We'll talk about it."

As our conversations continued over the next few weeks, Robert and I both worried. What about our busy lifestyle, my love of indoor cats, or the expense of adopting dogs with potential health problems? Although most adoptions are done through agencies, we were starting from scratch, heading for experiences unknown to us. My usual response to uncertainty, however, is to do research. I began calling vets and learned the cost of various procedures. I read books, looked up articles, and generally became obsessed with the idea of owning one of these wonderful creatures. After several weeks, we realized the idea wouldn't go away and made the call to our friend. She told us the owner she worked with had three dogs available. Although they were personal favorites, none of them could make it as runners. One dog had been kept far longer than usual because the owner liked her and hated to put her down. At eighteen months the three littermates were already washed up and out of the business. Our friend promised a delivery when she had homes arranged for the other two.

We set about getting ready for the first needy "baby" in our home. I chose my vet carefully after finding one nearby who had actually worked in the racing kennels in California. His partner had worked there too. What a stroke of luck to have two greyhound familiar vets in one office. I read Branigan's book again, and we fenced in the back yard of our country home. I bought treats and talked with my vet about dog food and what sorts of problems to expect. To this day I am an info-fanatic with all sorts of "greyhound goodies" file folders.

Finally the big day arrived! Our friend called us to meet her at the front of our property. Robert rushed out, without so much as a backward glance at me as I finished dressing. When I reached her van I was utterly amazed. They were the prettiest things I had ever seen! Every time they would turn their heads they would try to kiss each other through their muzzles. A car sped by and the big male spun around to place himself between the danger and the two females behind him. They had obviously bonded to each other during the trip after being isolated for so much of their lives, but we sorted them out finally to hear their stories. Stubby, a fawn female, was so named because her tail had been caught in a door when she was just a pup, leaving it a few inches shorter. She had never made it past her training races, but had been kept by the owner for six more months. Angel, the big red brindle male, immediately seemed to want my complete attention and was very reluctant to move away. Sunshine, a tiny red fawn female, seemed to wiggle all the time and had to get her nose on everything around her. Although she had been fast on the track, she had been far more interested in playing with all the other dogs and had caused a few accidents.

Now, all we had to do was pick the one we wanted. It seemed like an easy task. But Robert was looking at me with big moon eyes and pitiful appeals. He liked the friendly little wiggle-butt, Sunshine, the best. Yet, here I had this big strapping tiger-striped dog doing his best to wrap himself around my legs. The worst part of all was the way they cried and struggled when we separated them from each other. Our friend looked at me once and said gently, "Do you really *want* to separate them?" The idea hadn't even occurred to us but the possibility came in a blinding flash. You guessed it already—all of a sudden we were the proud owners of three rescued racing greyhounds! There was no way in the world any of those dogs were getting back in that van.

We are very lucky, because our story has the very best of endings. It could have turned out much differently. I had done my research well and knew ahead of time what would be required. We have four acres of land, and no children to need attention. We own an antique store and I teach school so we can afford the additional expenses. We didn't have the advantage of the services offered by an adoption group, but we were working directly with the trainer who knew the dogs well enough to pick some for us. In the end, the money and concern never came close to the joy and wonder they brought to our home. Multiple adoptions have the advantage that the dogs keep each other company and learn from the rewards given to the others. Although we started with mostly "outside" dogs (South Carolina is very mild), they were so easy to get along with that they soon became part of the house whenever we were home. We didn't even have chewing and house-training problems after the rules were reinforced a bit. The cat soon learned that they were bigger than she was and the dogs in turn learned that although that furry thing was really aggravating, mommy and daddy wouldn't let you eat it. Of course we had to take things slowly and learned along with the dogs mostly by trial and error. Every second was worth it. Never in my life have I known dogs who work their way so quickly into your heart. They must love being with us too. One night my husband woke in the middle of the night and was horrified to find the back door on the "dog porch" (their sleeping spot) had blown wide open. Judging by the leaves inside, it had been that way for some time. All three dogs were curled up together asleep, however, less than two feet from freedom Our hearts skipped several beats, but we took our luck that night as a good sign from above.

Have you guessed yet which dog became our favorite? She is always quiet, loves nothing better than to sleep in the living room touching us. When she has the chance she runs the fastest. She always comes to us for attention first, even when there is food waiting. She is patient and will stand for the longest time (without being irritated) hoping to get a rub. Give her a rawhide bone and she won't touch another thing in the house. Take her in our shop and she walks straight to her rug before going to sleep, only moving if someone wants to pet her. If I could only have one, she would be it. The dog is Stubby, of course; the one we didn't want at first. She'll never feel lonely and forgotten again.

from GREYHOUND TALES

THE MEANING OF FORGIVENESS

"For it is in giving that we receive."

ST. FRANCIS OF ASSISI

Did you ever notice that animals don't hold a grudge? They're not like people in that regard. Forget to pick up your daughter's dress at the cleaner, or call your mother, or your kid brother's baseball game, and you're in big trouble. But get too busy to notice your dog standing in the doorway with a ball in his mouth, and your dog will quietly lie down until you're ready to play with him. No apology necessary—just a wag of the tail and eyes that say "Let's go!"

It's not that animals don't notice our flaws. They see them better than we do. It's just that they don't let our flaws interfere with their love for us.

Danny

PEG KEHRET

When Jessica Mitchell was three years old, she went to visit her grandmother. Her uncle was also visiting that day. He had brought along his dog, a pit bull.

Pit bull terriers, commonly known as pit bulls, were originally bred to fight. Although pit bulls can be gentle, many are used as guard dogs and are sometimes trained to be aggressive.

As little Jessica ran up the sidewalk toward her grandmother's house, her uncle's dog attacked her. Jessica screamed with pain and fear as the dog knocked her down and bit her many times in the face and around her eyes.

Police and paramedics raced to the scene. Sirens wailing, an ambulance rushed Jessica to the hospital.

She went immediately into surgery, where doctors rebuilt her torn cheek and put her jaw muscle back together. Jessica spent a week in the hospital. Her wounds were painful, but eventually they healed, leaving a lot of scar tissue.

When Jessica was in first grade, she was hospitalized again while doctors did reconstructive surgery to minimize a C-shaped scar around one eye. Later, another surgery removed excess scar tissue from her jaw. While her face looks fine, she may still need further surgery.

After she was attacked, Jessica became fearful of dogs. She

liked other animals, and she understood that most dogs never attack anyone unless they are threatened themselves. Still, whenever she saw a dog, she felt panicky.

By the time Jessica was eight, she wanted to conquer her fear. Many of her friends had dogs, and Jessica longed to pet them and play with them without being frightened.

She didn't think she would feel threatened by a little puppy, so she asked her parents if she could have one. Mr. and Mrs. Mitchell agreed, and they took Jessica to the Humane Society.

One of the available puppies that day was a shepherd/Lab mix who was eight weeks old. Because he was brought to the shelter when he was too young to be adopted, he had been placed in a foster home, where he had received plenty of love and attention.

The pup was gentle and friendly and liked being held. The Humane Society staff thought he would be a good choice for Jessica, and Jessica thought so, too. She named him Danny and took him home.

Danny turned out to be the perfect puppy. His silliness made Jessica laugh. She liked to pet him and play with him. Danny gave her puppy kisses and napped on her lap.

Of course he grew bigger, but Jessica already loved and trusted him. She had nothing to fear, even when he was fully grown. Although the rest of Jessica's family enjoyed Danny, too, he seemed to know that he was Jessica's dog.

While she felt completely comfortable with Danny, Jessica still had twinges of fear when she met other dogs.

A year after she adopted Danny, Jessica joined 4-H, an international program for young people. The 4-H club emblem is a four-leaf clover. The four Hs stand for head, heart, hands, and health.

All 4-H members select a project to work on. Jessica could choose from dozens of possible subjects, including plant science, computers, performing arts, geology, and woodworking. Because Jessica was having so much fun with Danny, she chose "Companion Animals."

At weekly meetings, Jessica learned about vaccinations Danny needed, how to groom him, and how to control parasites such as fleas, ticks, and lice. She and Danny practiced basic obedience. He learned how to heel on a leash, how to stay, and how to follow other commands.

As they worked together, Jessica and Danny became even closer; each one trusted the other completely.

Of course, the other members of Jessica's 4-H dog group brought their dogs to the weekly meetings. Jessica got to know those dogs well and grew to like and trust them. Before long, she was no longer afraid of dogs.

Jessica also took a 4-H veterinary science class. She learned more about the health of her dog and became aware of career opportunities for working with animals.

Jessica's family had a fenced backyard with a locked gate so that Danny could spend time outdoors. One afternoon, the Mitchells left Danny in the backyard while they were away for a while.

Before, whenever they returned home, Danny had always run to greet them, happily wagging his tail. That day, when the family got home, Danny tried to hide behind a bush. Instead of flapping his tail from side to side as he usually did, he kept it tucked between his legs. He shook with fear.

The Mitchells took Danny inside and examined him carefully, but they couldn't find anything wrong. Jessica knew something had happened, but she had no way to find out what. Danny did not seem sick; he seemed terrified.

From then on, whenever anyone outside the family came to the door, Danny hid under the dining room table, peeking nervously out at the visitor.

Jessica's formerly happy dog was now a fearful dog, and she had no idea why. Jessica gave him extra love and attention, as did her parents, but Danny continued to act frightened of strangers.

About this time one of the local utility companies was doing work in the Mitchells' neighborhood. A few days after Danny began acting scared, a worker from the utility company needed to go into the Mitchells' yard.

Danny was outside. Though he had been cowering at strangers, he barked ferociously at this man.

Jessica's father went to get Danny, to put him inside.

The worker said, "It's okay. If he gets near me, I'll just Mace him."

Mr. Mitchell knew that Mace, a chemical spray, is sometimes used to control mobs of people who are rioting. When Mace is sprayed in a person's face, it causes tears, dizziness, and nausea. The victim is usually temporarily unable to move.

Horrified, the Mitchells speculated about what might have happened on the day they were gone. Utility workers had been working in the neighborhood then, too. Had one of them climbed the fence to do work in the yard and then, when Danny approached, sprayed the dog with Mace? If so, it was no wonder Danny acted traumatized. And no wonder he was now afraid of everyone except his family.

Danny continued to act scared of everyone who came into Jessica's house. But when she took him to the 4-H meetings, he was excited and seemed happy to go. He acted glad to see the other dogs, and he clearly enjoyed the 4-H training.

Just as 4-H had been a way for Jessica to forget her fear of dogs she didn't know, 4-H became a way for Danny to get over his fear of people he didn't know.

In between 4-H meetings, Jessica and Danny practiced all the obedience commands over and over. When Danny obeyed correctly, Jessica praised him or rewarded him with a small treat. Their practice sessions became a way to play together. Jessica kept records of his progress.

Danny did so well that Jessica decided it would be fun to show him in a 4-H dog show. Unlike most dog shows, 4-H shows do not require that the dogs be purebreds. In 4-H, the judging is based on the ability of the person showing the dog to control the dog and on the condition and grooming of the dog. A mixed breed like Danny has just as much chance of winning as a purebred does.

Jessica established a goal for herself and Danny: to compete in the 4-H dog show at the county fair. Before a 4-H member can show a dog at the fair, he or she must successfully complete two 4-H Fun Matches.

The Fun Matches are run like dog shows but are done just for practice, to get the dogs and their handlers accustomed to performing.

Jessica and Danny entered a 4-H Fun Match. The event was well-named; Jessica and Danny both had a great time. Danny loved being brushed and fussed over while Jessica waited for her turn to perform. Jessica liked watching the other 4-H kids and their dogs. Most of all, she enjoyed showing the judges how well Danny obeyed.

Danny heeled beautifully as he walked in with Jessica, sat down promptly on command, and stood motionless while the judge examined his fur.

The hardest part of the show for Danny was when the dogs were told to stay while the owners walked away from them. There were four dogs in Danny's group, and they were supposed to sit where they were until the judge told the owners to call them.

Jessica knew Danny wanted to be close to her when there were strangers present. After she gave him the stay command, she crossed her fingers while she went to the far side of the arena. Danny sat still, with his eyes focused on Jessica. Even when one of the other dogs got up before he was supposed to and ran to his owner, Danny remained where he was. When Jessica finally told him to come, Danny galloped happily to her side.

"Good dog," she told him. "Good, good dog!"

To Jessica's delight, she and Danny won second place. She received a rainbow-colored ribbon with a rosette.

Jessica entered another Fun Match, and this time she received a first-place blue ribbon. She and Danny continued to practice. She groomed him daily.

They moved up to the novice class and then to graduate novice, where Danny had to know more difficult commands and be able to do them without a leash. They entered another match and another. They won more ribbons. Jessica and Danny made it to the county fair where they did so well that they qualified to go on to the state fair. There, the top two handlers each won a medallion with dogs on it. Jessica beamed with pride as the judge hung the beautiful medallion on its red-white-and-blue ribbon around her neck.

The crowd watching would never have imagined that this confident girl, who showed Danny with such poise, had once been terrified of dogs.

A vendor at the fair sold necklaces. One was a silver chain with a four-leaf clover on it. Purchasers could have their names engraved on the clover. Jessica bought a necklace, and she had two names engraved on it: Jessica and Danny.

He had rescued her from her fear of dogs, and she had rescued him from his fear of people. No wonder they are best friends now.

from SHELTER DOGS

Coming Home

DAVID REDDING

I remember coming home from the navy after World War II. Home was so far out in the country that when we went hunting, we had to go toward town. We had moved there for my father's health when I was thirteen. We raised cattle and horses.

This is how I got Teddy, a big, black Scottish shepherd. Teddy was my dog, and he would do anything for me. He waited for me to come home from school. He slept beside me, and when I whispered he ran to me even if he was eating. At night, no one could get within half a mile without Teddy's permission. During those long summers in the fields I would only see the family at night. I did not know how to leave him. How do you explain to someone who loves you that you are leaving him and will not be chasing woodchucks with him tomorrow as always?

So, coming home from the navy that first time was something I can scarcely describe. The last bus stop was fourteen miles from the farm, but I knew every step of the way. Suddenly Teddy heard me and began his warning barking. Then I whistled—only once. The barking stopped. There was a yelp of recognition, and I knew that a big black form was hurtling toward me in the darkness. Almost immediately he was there in my arms. To this day, that is the best way I can explain what I mean by "coming home."

What comes home to me now is the eloquence with which that unforgettable memory speaks to me of God. If my dog, without any explanation, would love me and run to take me back after all that time, would not my God?

from THE GOLDEN STRING

Coco, Spot and Orph the Dwarf

DON MACHHOLZ

Coco came to us in a cardboard box one summer day in 1980. He was an English Angora rabbit with tassels at the end of his ears. It wasn't my idea to have a rabbit for a pet. Laura, my wife, learned of a litter that was being divided up and quickly warmed to the idea of our taking him on. Since we are both animal lovers, it was okay by me.

Getting to know Coco was more fun than I had expected. Coco's breed is generally raised for its hair (no pun intended), so his long hair had to be clipped every few months. After initial objections, Coco learned to settle down for the hour-long session while I held him and Laura did the cutting.

In no time he became a patient rabbit, and a playful one, too. For some reason he was attracted to any object waving in the air, and we developed a game. I'd wave a newspaper a few inches off the ground, and he would charge at it like a bull for a matador's cape. He'd charge at it, that is, if there were no strangers around. If I wanted him to show off for our guests, he'd eschew the game completely, and I'd stand there rattling the paper and feeling like a fool.

In the spring of 1981 we let Coco out of the cage full-time. With our fenced-in yard we had no fear that he would hop off, but soon a problem of a different nature arose. Coco began munching our garden. So we raised fences around certain plants and shrubs. We told Coco, "You may eat of any plant in the backyard, but you are not to touch the lemon tree, rose bushes, strawberry plants, geraniums, succulents, or anything in the vegetable garden." So what did that leave him? The lawn. Which he ate.

About this time, we bought Spot. We really didn't *need* another rabbit, but Laura said that since Coco was hers, I should have a rabbit, too. Spot was a French lop, a breed characterized by long ears that droop to the floor. When he was young he stepped on them as he hopped across our kitchen. He always managed to get at least one ear in his water dish as he drank. Spot's long ears and low posture and "hound dog" eyes made him look sad, but I was certain that this gentle, warmhearted rabbit was not unhappy about anything—especially about being with us.

After a few weeks we transferred him to the backyard to roam and nibble with Coco. Contrary to nature, our two male rabbits got along very well. Once set free, Spot often came up with a case of sore paws—a result of his constant digging, an exercise he learned from Coco. When his feet hurt, he moved with a slow, rolling hop, giving the impression of a real "cool" character.

Spot, it turned out, liked to perform before company. I'd put him on the picnic table, then stoop down a foot from the table edge. When I called to him, he would leap onto my shoulder. On Halloween he went to a costume party with me.

I was a lion tamer, and he was the lion, wearing a mane and executing perfectly his trick of jumping from the top of his portable cage to my shoulder.

In December of 1981 we acquired a third rabbit, one whose owner had to give her up. Her name was Orphan. A Netherlands dwarf rabbit, she soon became "Orph the Dwarf" or just Orph. We had her spayed, then released her to be with Coco and Spot. She was smaller than they, but restless and independent.

The three of them never fought. Instead, they seemed to look out for one another. Each evening our silent pets could be seen on our patio, gazing into the night like children staring out into the rain. Warm days would find them under the shade trees; on wet days they'd be in or under their cage.

Then in the autumn of 1982, still another rabbit joined the group, a birthday gift from Laura to me. This one, a French lop, I named Flopsy. She was only six weeks old, and we decided to raise her in our kitchen during the winter, then mate her with Spot in the spring. By now, since Laura and I didn't want the rabbits to dig up our lawn any further, we had confined them to an area on the south side of the yard by constructing a short fence a few feet inside our large wooden fence. We chose the far, south side of the yard because our neighbors to the north had two large dogs.

A few days before Christmas a storm was moving into our area. But the weather was calm and sunny when I fed the rabbits, pausing to give Spot a chunk of carrot. As I was driving to work, the wind came up, and then rain began to fall. I trusted that the rabbits would take cover in their cage as usual. . . .

But in the afternoon a call came from Laura. "Don," she said in a breaking voice, "I g-got out of w-work early and—

and—" Then she was crying so hard I could only make out the words "fence . . . dogs . . . rabbits." Within seconds I was on my way to the parking lot.

When I pulled into our driveway, Laura was waiting for me. I wrapped my arms around her and drew her close. Looking over her shoulder into our backyard, I could see what had happened. The strong winds had blown down the north fence, and the neighbor's dogs had entered our yard and attacked the rabbits.

The rain continued, running down my face and soaking into my clothes as I walked forward. I found Spot first, lying near the area where he used to wait for the first rays of the warm morning sun. His body was cold and muddy and lifeless. Coco lay dead in the garden, with a broken neck. I did not find Orph until I went into our neighbor's yard and looked into his garage. The dogs were cowering there, for they knew I was angry. Orph was dead on the garage floor.

"Comfort ye, comfort ye my people," said the prophet Isaiah. The shock was severe; the sorrow left us wordless. I read my own thoughts in Laura's eyes. We were not there when our silent pets needed us most. Yet we were responsible for them, and they had depended upon us. And could we really blame the dogs, who were only following their inborn instinct?

That evening Laura and I sat together for a long time in silence. Then Laura spoke. She was groping for understanding. "After a loss, God gives back to you," she said.

I nodded slowly. This was not a new idea to us. We had talked about it often before and explored it in our Sunday school class. Now we had to believe that this was so. But when you are sorrowing, even these things you believe in can be hard to accept.

Christmas Eve was my day off. I was up long before dawn to spend a few hours on my hobby, stargazing through my telescope from a nearby mountain. I came home at 7:00 A.M. and headed straight for the shower. Then I dressed and went to the kitchen to make a cup of coffee. Halfway across the room I paused. Something was different. But what? Some kind of presence. Strange. I looked around. Flopsy, I noticed, had hopped out of the sleeping box we had made for her. Now, in the quiet room, I heard faint sounds, soft noises coming from Flopsy's empty box. I tiptoed to the box, knelt down and looked inside. Nestled in the paper shavings were three . . . baby rabbits.

"Laura," I called in a voice rising with excitement. "Laura, come and see something you won't believe."

We had not even known Flopsy was pregnant. Now, looking back, I remembered that we had brought Spot into the house to treat his sore paws around Thanksgiving. But at that time Flopsy was not even three months old, an age generally considered too young to conceive. . . .

With the assurance of things hoped for, Laura and I built a sturdy new fence in our backyard for Flopsy and her three French lops, Spreckles, Mopsy and Ink Spot.

Ladybug

GARY RICHMOND

When I was seven our family got a small black and tan puppy and named her Ladybug. I do not recall where we got her, but even after more than 30 years have come and gone I can vividly recall the warmth of her head lying across my bare feet and the look of love in her eyes as she watched to see if she would be invited on any adventure that led her beyond the boundaries of our yard. She was an ardent traveler and loved to ride in the car. No dog ever born enjoyed more the wind whipping her ears and flapping her lips as she leaned as far as we would permit out the back window of our '53 Chevrolet station wagon.

Ladybug weighed in at about 15 pounds, maybe 20, and the consensus was that she was a cross between a cocker spaniel and a beagle. She was a happy dog and ticklish. If you scratched her in just the right place she actually smiled. Now I know that's hard to believe, but, hang it all, she smiled, and if you saw it you would call it that too.

When I was young I actually thought of Ladybug as a member of the family. To me she was the youngest child, Ladybug Richmond. She slept with us, and many was the morning that I was licked awake. Between the ages of seven and nine I never washed my ears because Ladybug did it for me almost every morning.

She did have a fault that remained with her all the days of her life. She had breath that you could see on a warm day. Whatever doggy breath is, she had twice as much as should be allotted. We had to apologize for it more than once. She was also possessed of a great capacity for natural gas production and could not contain it.

Ladybug was my friend and shadow and I always loved her—but never more than the one summer day that I asked for and obtained her forgiveness. Here is what happened.

I was raised in Altadena, California, a small friendly town nestled against the San Gabriel Mountains. You have seen these very mountains if you have watched the Rose Parade or the Rose Bowl football game. The San Gabriels watch over Pasadena and Altadena and most of the Los Angeles basin. Now Altadena had much to commend it, but right up there at the top, smack dab in the middle of the "amen corner" was Kern's Delicatessen. Old Mr. Kern had located some of the finest culinary delights known to the palates of our species. His Swiss cheese, pumpernickel bread, and kosher dill pickles were the best. It was a four-block walk to the deli, but I would make the walk anytime some benefactor would finance the pilgrimage.

One very hot summer afternoon in deep August I had a little extra cash and remembered how much I enjoyed biting into one of Mr. Kern's renowned kosher dills. I was with a friend, Doug Sigler, and asked if he would like to walk to Kern's with me. As it turned out, my brother and a friend of his decided to go also. When we got to the front door of our house, Ladybug was wiggling with delight for she was sure we were going to let her come along. After a little banter we agreed and were out the door on our way to the gates of heaven.

Ladybug was not leashed because she would never bite

anyone. She was always bounding just ahead, stopping now and then to smell something and make a memory. She would run over and jump on us now and then to let us know she was glad to be part of the adventure. Ladybug was five going on six at the time, and I was going into the seventh grade in the fall.

When we arrived at Kern's, we told Ladybug to sit at the front door and wait for us while we ate inside. I purchased one piece of his pumpernickel bread, one slice of aged Swiss cheese, one large kosher dill pickle, and a bottle of Dad's Old-Fashioned Root Beer. Life doesn't get better than eating at Kern's Delicatessen with family and friends. We left only after licking our fingers clean; leaving anything uneaten would have been a sin.

Once outside we ordered Ladybug to follow us home. Twenty steps down the street we looked into the Hillcrest Pharmacy window and noticed the latest issue of *Mad* magazine. We again ordered Ladybug to sit on the sidewalk and wait while we went into the store. We read *Mad* over my friend's shoulder and laughed at the absurd humor. Laughter's tears streamed down our faces. The store clerk asked us to buy or fly, so we left. We left a little embarrassed and miffed. We also left through the back door, which provided a shortcut home. Ladybug, however, continued to wait patiently at the front door of Hillcrest Pharmacy.

On the way home we groused over being given the bum's rush at the pharmacy. The afternoon began to blend with evening, and our friends both left for home and dinner. My dad came home from a hard day's work in construction and, after washing up, called us to the dinner table. It was a meat-and-potatoes meal and we had a lot of the kind of leftovers a family dog would kill for. My father scraped them onto a plate and stepped out the back door to call for Ladybug.

She didn't come.

Dad came back into the house and asked Steve and me if we had seen her, and we both looked at each other. I didn't know for sure what Steve was going to do, but I was trying to figure out a way to blame our thoughtless mistake on him. I refused to answer, hoping that if my brother spoke first he would get most of the blame for losing our dog. Steve finally admitted that we had left her outside the pharmacy. My Dad had a disgusted look, which he administered pretty equally as I remember. He told us to jump in the car, and we backed out of our driveway a lot faster than usual. He didn't say much, but he did inquire if we had traded our brains for sawdust. We knew well that we had better not answer that particular question. If we said no, we were smart-mouthing. If we said yes, we were smart-mouthing. So we both did what he wanted us to do; we looked guilty and stupid and kept quiet. (Now I don't know what you're thinking, but I don't agree with the notion that there are no appropriate times for a tongue-lashing. God did it all the time to Israel, and Jesus did it to His disciples. Steve and I were getting less than we deserved, and I knew it even then.)

My father knew enough about dogs to know that Ladybug was capable of following her own scent home, so he followed the route we had walked to the delicatessen. The farther we drove without seeing her the worse I felt. I had let down one of my best friends and I knew it. I had a lump in my throat as I began to picture my dog run over by a car or cringing in the back of a cage at the dog pound. We finally rounded the corner of Mariposa Lane and Lake Street and saw a small dark form curled into a ball by the front door of the pharmacy. Steve stuck his head out the window and yelled, "Here, girl!"

His yell awoke Ladybug, and she bounced against the glass

thinking we were still in the store. Steve left the car and picked her up.

I have never witnessed a more emotional reunion. Ladybug wiggled until I thought she would fall apart. She whined happily all the way home and licked every hand that came within a foot of her.

My father, happy about the outcome, said, "All's well that ends well, but don't you two ever let that happen to your dog again. I don't have to tell you all the bad things that could have happened to her, do I?" We nodded.

That night I asked Ladybug if she wanted to sleep with me. Her tail wagged as she ran ahead of me and jumped up on the bed. When I turned out the light, I called her to come close and I hugged her and told her how sorry I was to have let her down. She just kissed me and rolled over to have me scratch her tummy. I did that until we both fell asleep.

Ladybug was always anxious to forgive. Her only desire was that she be part of a family, our family, her family. The saying that dogs are man's best friends really isn't so far off in my experience.

from IT'S A JUNGLE OUT THERE

When Daddy Decided to Splurge

ROBERTA L. MESSNER

$\mathcal{A}$ friend was going to look after my dog, Muffin, while I went into the hospital for some surgery. On the way to her house I stopped to see my mom and dad, Muffin trotting in after me as though she were a regular member of the family. A Benji look-alike, she'd been my soul mate for seven years. From the first time I'd spotted the wiry-haired stray hiding in the briers by a chain-link fence, we'd been inseparable. I'd always tried to give her the best life I could.

"Muffin will be just fine while you're gone," Mom assured me.

"I can't believe you're not putting that mongrel up at the Hilton," Dad commented. "The way you spoil her! Giving her that fancy-dancy stocking full of dog biscuits at Christmastime and taking her everywhere."

I steeled myself against his words. That I spent too much money on Muffin was an old issue. That I should be saving for a rainy day was an even older argument.

"I've always told myself," Dad went on, "that I'd be better off if I were Roberta's dog."

I just hugged Muffin a little harder and tried to ignore Dad's remarks. But even after I left, they stung. I dropped Muffin off at my friend's and drove on to the hospital, still thinking of what Dad had said. Why did his criticism hurt so much? I was a grown woman with a successful career as a nurse. Why did his approval matter? It was as though I were a little girl again, trying to make my daddy proud.

A child of the Depression, Dad had had to be careful with money. He'd worked as a telegraph operator on the railroad and supplemented his earnings selling old pocket watches at flea markets. A horse trader, people called him. When I was barely out of diapers, I picked up his jargon. He loved to tell about the time he tugged on my pigtails and asked if I'd take a five-dollar bill for my Tiny Tears doll. I took a long look at her pink bottle and packet of tissues and shot back, "I want more, this here's a rare one!"

By the time I was 10 years old, I was doing odd jobs in the neighborhood, hoping to match Dad's industry. I hosed off porch furniture, waxed floors and starched the curtains in a neighbor's guest bedroom.

With the first dollar I earned, I put aside 10 percent for church, but the next 10 cents I took straight to Broughton's Dairy. There I bought a double-dip cone of lime sherbet, Daddy's favorite, and climbed the steep iron stairs of the telegraph tower where he worked.

I tapped on the screen door and hollered, "Surprise!" I just knew he'd be pleased. "I bought this for you with the money I've been making." Lime-green sherbet dripped down my fingers as Daddy tapped out a Morse code message.

Finally he looked up and smiled. But as he took a lick of soupy sherbet, he cautioned, "Don't be squandering all your hard-earned money on ice cream now. You should be putting something away for the future."

All the way home I fought back tears. Wasn't there anything I could do to make him happy? When I was a little older I took up the violin so I could join in when he pulled out his fiddle. Then I studied piano. My first recital, I knew how proud he'd be of the way I played "The Londonderry Air." But at the last minute Daddy couldn't come. He had to work overtime. We needed the money. For a rainy day.

After I studied nursing and pursued my RN career, I became something of a horse trader myself, going to flea markets, collecting antiques. No matter what I bought, Dad was able to take the wind out of my sails when I told him the deal I'd made or how much I'd managed to save.

With Muffin, though, I never cut corners. She deserved the very best. In the hospital after my surgery, I kept thinking of how happy I'd be to see her again.

It was then that I received word Muffin had jumped the fence in my friend's backyard and raced off. No one could find her. Lying in my hospital bed, I prayed that whatever happened, she would be safe. Still, when no news came, I was frantic.

The morning my mother drove me home from the hospital, all I saw were dogs. Dogs playing, dogs barking, dogs running to greet their masters. But no wagging tail awaited me when I got home.

"I'm so sorry, Roberta," Mom said, tucking a blanket around me on the sofa. "Your father is worried too."

Yeah, right, I thought, scrunching miserably into the pillow. Later, I got up to make a cup of tea, and the phone rang. The caller said she'd seen the ad about Muffin and wanted me to know she'd just lost her little pooch and knew exactly how I felt.

The ad? I wondered groggily before stumbling back to rest.

The next night I got more calls. One man who worked at the Waffle House asked for a better description of Muffin. Before hanging up he added, "Your dad must think the world of you to go to all this trouble." Why did he say that? Another caller said, "The dog your father described to me is here, I'm sure of it." What were they talking about?

The following day a coworker drove me around to check on the leads I'd received. None of the shaggy mutts people had found were Muffin. One was 100 miles away, but I knew how Muffin loved to jump into any open car door, so I felt compelled to investigate. Alas, the "female dog with matted hair" turned out to be a male cat. "I felt so bad for you I guess I got carried away," the stranger admitted.

Then my sister called. "I found Muffin at the pound!" I was beside myself with relief as I went with her to investigate. But I knew at once when I approached the cage that the thin, mangy dog wasn't my Muffin.

"Just call her name," my sister urged. "Maybe she's lost weight."

"Muffin!" I cried. And from the saddest corridor in the animal world, 56 dogs of every description howled in unison.

With that my heart just broke. All those animals longing for a home expressed my own longing for my dog. It was as though my loneliness had found a voice.

That night another stranger called. She wanted me to know she was praying for me. "I don't know why this had to happen to you, honey," she said, "but God knows how you feel. Trust him with your sadness."

By then I had given up, but when one more person called, absolutely certain he had my dog, I allowed myself to hope one more time. A friend drove me to the end of a muddy hollow, where a man stood with a yelping, stubby-tailed orange dog much bigger than Muffin. "She just has to be yours," he insisted as the huge dog pawed my skirt.

"I don't think so," I said sadly.

The man looked at me woefully. "Lady," he said, "I've already promised my grandkids a trip to Disney World with all that reward money your father's giving."

I was stunned. "Reward?" From the man who always accused me of squandering money on Muffin? The thrifty father who wanted me to save for a rainy day?

"I got the ad right here." He pulled out the beat-up newspaper he had jammed in his back pocket. "See, this one." He held out the want ads and pointed to an item he'd circled.

I took the paper, read it once, then twice, blinking hard to clear the tears that blurred my vision. The ad was clear and to the point. "Please help me find my baby girl's lost dog," it said. "$1,000 reward."

"Thank you anyway," I said in a wobbly voice. "Do you mind if I keep this newspaper?"

Mom and Dad visited me that night. "Daddy," I said, "you and I have some things to talk about."

That's when Mom spilled the beans: "He's been looking everywhere for Muffin. He gets in the car and drives all over, calling out the window. And he's been telling people to call and to pray for you."

I couldn't believe my ears. Now I had to ask him about the biggest surprise of all. "Daddy," I said, "what about the reward money?"

He shuffled his feet. "Well," he said, "I figured it was the only way that dog could be found."

"But a thousand dollars? Daddy, that's so much money!

You've never splurged like that. What about always saving for a rainy day?"

Daddy fixed his eyes on a crack in his brown leather sole. "Sweetheart," he said, "the day you lost your little Muffin I felt the biggest downpour of my life. You were so sad, I would have given anything to get your dog back for you. I'm sorry she hasn't come home."

I thought of all the scrimping and saving Dad must have done to put away a thousand dollars and how quick he was now to give it up for me. The years suddenly faded, and I was once more the girl who had learned bargaining from the best horse trader in the business. You can't put a dollar figure on love, but Dad had come up with "a rare one" of his own. Nothing was too much for my happiness.

"Thank you, Dad," I said, my voice breaking.

This story has a bittersweet ending. Muffin never turned up, but my prayers that she was okay did a lot to comfort me. Eventually, Dad took me back to the pound, and I brought home one of those howling mutts that was yearning for a home. It wasn't a replacement for my lost dog—nothing could take the place of Muffin—but this was a new dog to spoil to my heart's content. I named her Cleo, and we had many happy years together. And from that point on, Dad and I had an understanding. He can complain all he wants about the money I spend, and I can spoil my dog as much as I want.

Love can express itself in many different ways. I realize that when I was young, Daddy worked hard to be a good provider, saving for a rainy day. Then, as now, he was sheltering his baby girl, and giving me love the best way he knew how.

GROWING PAINS

"*Our animals shepherd us through certain eras of our lives.*"

ANONYMOUS

There's something about bringing up an animal that helps us to grow up, too. And sometimes it's hard to tell which one is the teacher. Perhaps it works both ways: as we teach a young animal to adapt to our ways, the animal teaches us the ways of loyalty, responsibility, understanding and love.

Whatever the animal's age, and whatever ours may be, we can learn much from each other.

Caesar, Brutus and St. Francis

SUE MONK KIDD

"I'm taking you guys to church, so please try to behave, okay?" Our two rambunctious young beagles, Caesar and Brutus, sat on the front seat of the car and ignored me, their floppy ears perked to attention as they watched the stream of traffic. At the stoplight, I braked as a woman walked her black poodle across the street. Caesar and Brutus let out a string of woo-woo-woofs.

"Now see? That's what I mean," I told them. "None of that."

It was a balmy October afternoon and we were on our way to a "Blessing of the Animals" service at Grace Episcopal Church. I'd never attended one of these services, and frankly, I had no idea what to expect. I only knew it was held each year on St. Francis Day (since St. Francis had a special love for animals) and that folks were invited to bring their pets. From the moment I'd read about it, I'd had a nudging feeling I should go.

Now I wondered if I was out of my mind. What if Caesar and Brutus disrupted the service? It would be just like them. Beagles are bred to do three things: sniff, bark and charge at anything furry. Once my son found Caesar in our fenced backyard stranded up in a crepe myrtle tree where he'd *climbed* after a squirrel.

Earlier in the day I'd asked my children if they would like to come along to see the dogs blessed. "Let me get this straight," said Bob. "You're taking *our* dogs to church to get blessed with a lot of other animals?" He was biting the inside of his mouth to keep from laughing. Ann had simply gazed at me with her when-are-you-checking-into-the-asylum look.

I looked at the dogs, thumping their tails on the car seat, barking at everything that moved outside the car. "Will you be quiet?" I cried. The truth is, I'd never taken to these two hyperactive beagles the way I had to our beloved old, slow-moving spaniel, Captain. He'd presided quietly over the house for 13 years before he died. These two were his so-called "replacements." Some replacements.

I turned into the church parking lot just as the service was about to begin. Beside the children's playground was a table draped in white with a St. Francis statue on it. A little crescent of children, adults, dogs (*quiet* dogs) and other animals had formed around it. I lashed Caesar's and Brutus's leashes to my wrists like a rodeo cowboy getting ready to ride into the ring.

The dogs came out of the car in a yapping frenzy, noses to the ground, dragging me behind them. I tugged and wrestled them over to the other animals. The priest was saying something about celebrating the presence of animals on earth, how they too were part of God's wonderful plan.

"Woo-woo-woof! Woo-woo-woof!" they barked and bayed at the other dogs, drowning out the voice of the priest. People looked at me and smiled sympathetically. Even the other dogs stared at me.

Caesar and Brutus then spotted a pet carrier on the ground

to my left. Sitting regally behind the wire was a cat. "Woo-woo-woof!" They lunged toward the cat, nearly tipping me over. The priest was practically shouting now. I frantically tried to hush them as they strained on their leashes, which were cutting into my wrists to the point of pain. *Lord, what a disaster!* I thought. My children were right. This was a dumb idea. *Just wait till I get you two home.* I wanted to leave, but something—I don't know what—held me there.

The priest moved from one animal to the next, patting their heads, saying something to each one. Finally he stopped in front of my two disturbers of the peace and asked their names. "Caesar and Brutus," I replied in the most apologetic tone possible.

He touched their heads and smiled. "Bless you, Caesar and Brutus. We're thankful for your enthusiasm about life, for the joyful noise you make in response to it. May God watch over you and protect you."

Next we read in unison the famous prayer of St. Francis, our words filtering through the aria of my dogs' unending barking: "Lord, make me an instrument of Thy peace . . . "

Finally, mercifully, it was over.

Back home I opened the gate, let Caesar and Brutus into the backyard, then trudged into the kitchen, muttering.

"What happened?" asked my husband, Sandy.

"Those fool dogs practically ruined the St. Francis Day service. They acted like animals."

"They *are* animals," he pointed out.

For days I refused to let them in the house, where they usually slept. I scolded them for the least thing: for the limbs they dragged onto the deck, for turning over my Boston fern, for scratching at the door, but mostly for barking. They responded by wagging their tails and dropping a ball in front of me, hoping I would toss it. I would not.

Five days after the St. Francis Day disaster I happened to glance out the window and see the neighbor's cat sashaying along the back fence. An eerie feeling came over me. Why weren't the dogs barking? I stepped into the yard, into an awful, empty silence. With a thudding heart I peered at the gate. It was hanging open. Caesar and Brutus were gone.

I ran down the driveway, remembering Sandy's caution to keep the gate closed. "If those two dogs ever get out, I'm afraid they'll be long gone," he'd said. Had the meter reader come through it and left it ajar? Had the wind blown it open?

I hurried along the street calling their names. After scouring the neighborhood for two hours, I came home. There had been no sign of them. They had probably seen a squirrel and tracked it clear to North Carolina by now.

Sandy came home during lunch and we drove all over town. "If we ever find them, I'll never fuss at them again," I told Sandy.

He smiled at me. "I know."

After school the children joined the search. Late into the afternoon I kept stopping people on the street. "Have you seen two little beagles?" They all shook their heads.

As the day softened into dusk, we gave up and went home. I passed their dog bowls sitting empty in the kitchen and walked on into my study. I sat alone in the shadows and traced my finger along the edge of my desk. Suddenly I remembered how the priest put his hands on their heads. What had he said? *"Bless you, Caesar and Brutus. We're thankful for your enthusiasm for life. . . . May God watch over you and protect you."* I laid my head down and cried.

When I dried my eyes, it was dark out. I stood at the window and wondered if we would ever see them again. Just then a part of St. Francis's prayer came floating back into my head: " . . . *Where there is doubt, let me sow faith; where there is despair, hope . . . "* The words seemed full of urgency. I grabbed a flashlight and both dog leashes and headed out the door. "Where are you going?" Sandy asked.

"To sow faith and hope," I said.

I walked along the street, on and on, block after block.

"Woo-woo-woof!"

I froze. I would know that sound anywhere. I listened, following it until I came upon Caesar and Brutus sniffing through the garden in a stranger's yard. In the middle of the garden was a statue of St. Francis. Somehow I was not surprised.

As the dogs bounded into my arms and licked my face, I thanked God for St. Francis, who loved all creatures great and small, and was still teaching folks today to do the same. I thanked God for blessing my two beagles and for watching over them.

Back home I gave both dogs some milk and let them curl up on the foot of my bed. I rubbed their ears, feeling that great and piercing awareness that breaks in upon us at certain times in life, the awareness of not realizing how much you love the people or things close to you until you almost lose them.

I was suddenly filled with the need to seize every day and sow it full of all those wonderful things St. Francis prayed about: love and pardon, faith and hope, light and joy.

Sandy and the children appeared at the bedroom door. I went and put my arms around them. "I don't tell you enough," I said, "but I love you."

From the foot of the bed came a resounding "Woo-woo-woof."

Skiddor & Friends

GAYLE BUNNEY

They say that a person's pets often take on the personality of his or her owner, in which case I'm in serious trouble. They may lock me up. Because I don't have a single normal pet or horse on my property. Even my quarter horse stallion is not normal. Three Kits (herein referred to by his nickname, Skiddor) is sixteen hands high, an American Quarter Horse Association stallion who is bred for the track. His pedigree is a long list of champions, his conformation excellent, his potential as a sire great. So what's the problem? I'm afraid Skiddor thinks he is a dog. A very large dog. Thank heavens he is an outside dog, not a house dog or my problems would be a lot worse.

Let's start at the beginning. Once upon a time, I began searching for a new stallion prospect. My search took me far and wide, but no horse I looked at was good enough. Then one day I found him.

Having sustained a serious leg injury as a foal, he had been kept a stallion for his potential as a sire, even though he would never be able to race. He was raised properly on a large breeding farm. His first one and a half years were normal ones. He was a normal horse.

THEN HE CAME TO LIVE WITH ME. Things started out okay. Although he enjoyed the run of a two-acre paddock, he was lonely for companionship. This is where my husky/white shepherd cross dog comes into the picture. Blaze and Skiddor were just a couple of half-grown puppies, growing up together. They played tag. They ate together (yup, Blaze took a liking to rolled oats twice a day, when Skiddor was fed, both their heads buried in the feeder at the same time). They drank together, because regardless which one went to the water trough to drink, the other one was immediately also thirsty. I can't say they slept together though, because Blaze wasn't normal. He slept on the small BBQ table on the balcony, rain, snow or shine, it didn't matter, he slept on top of that table. By the time he was grown, his legs and head hung over the sides. Looked pretty uncomfortable to me, but then I've been known to sleep in some pretty weird places, too.

Blaze taught Skiddor to chew on sticks, a lost glove, plastic toys: basically nothing was safe from them. Their favourite game of all was Tug-a-War, Blaze on one end of an empty burlap sack, Skiddor on the other. Sometimes Skiddor would even let the smaller Blaze win. Then you would see an eighty-pound dog galloping across the pasture, dragging a thousand-pound colt behind him. Honest!

One bad thing though. Blaze taught Skiddor to chase cats. No cat is safe on this place. Skiddor never lays his ears back at anything or anybody. Except cats. He will leave his feed, even other horses to chase a cat. I have seen him stretched out flat, sleeping. A cat strolls by, he grunts and groans, gets to his feet and chases the cat under the nearest building or fence. Satisfied, he goes back to his resting place, relaxes, and is soon asleep again.

Skiddor is now two and a half years old with ten wives to his credit. He has a gentle old bred mare for companionship.

Blaze didn't take kindly to his buddy's interest in the opposite sex, his jealousy being so extreme that I was forced to give him away. Blaze may be gone but Skiddor still chews on anything and everything. His now six-acre pasture comes complete with enough fallen tree branches to keep him amused for hours. I have seen him pack an eight-foot branch around all afternoon, even though he steps on it and has a great deal of trouble getting it through the corral gate. No matter, he will pack them around like Blaze taught him to. Occasionally, I can't help myself and I will get an old feed sack and play a game of Tug-a-War with him. He sometimes lets me win too. Well, at least he never learned to bark at people. Well, not normal people anyway.

Skiddor must be seeing nothing but spots before his eyes now. On a sunny afternoon, wherever he looks, spots abound, because now I have a yard full of running, barking and playing Dalmatians. These beautiful dogs, which were bred long ago to be coach dogs, following their master's carriages, have a natural instinct to hang around the horses. The mares are not pleased with their presence, but the stallion welcomes them with happy snorts and playful jumps and leaps. His performance when they go visit him leaves other people convinced that he means to harm them, as he dances around them in his pasture. He would no more harm his friends than give up mares as his other favourite pastime. He places each hoof down with extraordinary care, even after a giant leap in the air, with a mighty backwards kick which would put the Lippizan stallions of Vienna to shame. Ears half back, he snakes his head towards them, his powerful jaws, which could crush the life from their bodies should he choose to do so, remaining firmly closed. Should one of them decide to take a rest in the deep, fresh straw of his covered shed, he is apt to approach them with gentle steps and doze beside the sleeping dog, sometimes even lying down and stretching his huge frame out beside them.

Such is the life for my best friends, these dogs and horses that share my home and bring me many hours of pleasure with their antics and joyful love of being alive. What more could I ever want?

from HORSE STORIES

A Simple Faith

DONNA CHANEY

Through the living room window I watched our 15-year-old son Jay trudge down the walk toward school. I was afraid that he might turn out into the snow-blanketed fields to hunt for his lost dog again. But he didn't. He turned, waved, then walked on, shoulders sagging.

His little beagle, Cricket, was missing.

Ten days had passed since that Sunday morning when Cricket did not return from his usual romp in the fields. Jay had worried all through Sunday school and church and, that afternoon, had roamed the countryside searching for his dog. At times, during those first anxious days, one or another of us would rush to the door thinking we had heard a whimper.

By now my husband Bill and I were sure Cricket had been taken by a hunter or struck by a car. But Jay refused to give up. One evening as I stepped outside to fill our bird feeder, I heard my son's plaintive calls drifting over the winter-blackened oaks and sycamores lining the fields near us. At last, he came in, stamped the snow off his boots, and said, "I know you think I'm silly, Mom, but I've been asking God about Cricket and I keep getting the feeling that he's out there somewhere."

Tears glistened in his blue eyes, and he ducked his head as he pulled off the boots.

I wanted to hold him close and tell him that he could easily get another dog. But I remembered too well the day four years before when we brought him his wriggling black-chocolate-and-white-colored puppy. The two of them had become inseparable. And though Cricket was supposed to sleep in the laundry room, it wasn't long before I'd find him peacefully snuggled on the foot of Jay's bed. He was such a lovable little fellow, I couldn't complain.

However, in the days since Cricket's disappearance, an unusually heavy snow had fallen. The temperatures were very low. I felt sure that no lost animal could have survived.

Besides, I had my own worries. Bill and I had just committed ourselves full time to a real-estate business venture. With skyrocketing mortgage interest rates, it was probably the worst time to be entering the field. I'd often lie awake at night worrying about it. Here we were in our late 40s, having sold a thriving dry-cleaning business, stepping into perilous waters.

Jay had helped his father remodel our new offices. And whenever he heard me express my concern, he'd glance up from his painting, smile and say: "Don't worry, Mom, the Lord is with you."

That was Jay, all right. We all attended church regularly; even so, Bill and I often wondered where he got his strong faith. Perhaps the blow of losing a much-loved older brother in an auto accident when he was six turned Jay to the Lord for help. In any case, I'd often find him in his room, reading the Bible, Cricket curled up at his feet.

Now a week and a half had passed since Cricket had disappeared. I told Jay that I felt there was such a thing as carrying hope too far.

Looking out the window, he said, "I know it seems impossible, Mom, with the snow and all. But Jesus said that a sparrow doesn't fall without God knowing it. And," he looked at the floor, "that must be true of dogs, too, don't you think?"

What could I do? I hugged him and sent him off to school. Then I drove over to our real-estate office where I forgot all about missing dogs in the hustle of typing up listings and answering the phone. The housing market seemed to be in more of a slump than ever, and mortgages were becoming an impossibility. I glanced over at my husband, who was trying to work out some kind of financial arrangement with a forlorn-looking young couple, and wondered if any of us would make it.

The phone rang. It was Jay.

"They let us out early, Mom—a teacher's meeting. I thought I'd hunt for Cricket."

My heart twisted.

"Jay," I tried to soften the irritation in my voice, "*please* don't put yourself through that anymore. The radio here says it's ten above zero, and you know there's no chance of . . . "

"But, Mom," he pleaded, "I have this feeling. I've got to try."

"All right," I sighed, "there's a pie I baked on the stove. Help yourself to some of it before you go."

I turned back to typing up the listings. Then a contract went through my typewriter before I realized that the afternoon sun had left our office window. I hoped Jay was back home now watching television or doing his homework.

But he wasn't at home. Instead, he was still out hunting for Cricket.

After our phone call, he had put on his boots and taken off through the field where he and Cricket used to go. He walked about a half-mile east and then heard some dogs barking in the distance. They sounded like penned-up beagles, so he headed in that direction. Crossing a bean field, he came upon a snowmobile someone had left sitting there. He looked it over and started walking again. But now, for some reason he couldn't determine, he found himself walking *away* from the barking.

Then he came to some railroad tracks. Hearing a train coming, he decided to watch it pass. The engineer waved at him as it roared by. With a boy's curiosity, he wondered if the tracks would be hot after a train went over them. So he climbed up the embankment and felt them; they were cold, of course.

Now, he didn't know what to do. He pitched a few rocks and finally decided to walk back down the tracks toward where he had heard the dogs barking earlier. As he stepped down the ties, the wind gusted and some hunters' shotguns echoed in the distance.

Then it happened.

Something made Jay stop dead still in his tracks. It seemed as if everything became quiet. And from down the embankment in a tangled fencerow came a faint sound, a kind of whimper.

Jay tumbled down the bank, his heart pounding. At the fencerow he pushed some growth apart and there was a pitifully weak Cricket, dangling by his left hind foot, caught in the rusty strands of the old fence. His front paws barely touched the ground, the snow around him was eaten away. It had saved him from dying of thirst.

My son carried him home and phoned me ecstatically.

Stunned, I rushed to the house. There in the kitchen was a very thin Cricket lapping food from his dish with a deliriously happy boy kneeling next to him.

Finishing, he looked up at Jay. In the little dog's adoring brown eyes I saw the innocent faith that had sustained him through those arduous days, the trust that someday his master would come.

I looked at my son who, despite all logic, went out with that same innocent faith and, with heart and soul open to his Master, was guided to his desire.

And I *knew* that if Bill and I, doing the best we could, walked in that same faith, we too would be guided through strange and circuitous paths. For how can anyone fail if he but heeds the words of the Prophet Isaiah: "And though the Lord give you the bread of adversity and the water of affliction, yet your Teacher will not hide Himself. . . . And your ears shall hear a word behind you, saying, 'This is the way, walk in it,' when you turn to the right or when you turn to the left." (Isaiah 30:20, 21, RSV)

Love Big Enough to Share

SHEILA M. PARDOE

"That was the strangest call," Dad said when he hung up the telephone at our Long Island home. "Someone at the railroad station says a crate just came in on the 4:12 addressed to me. When I asked him what it was, he got all huffy and told me to 'get down here immediately.'"

Mom and my three-year-old brother, Jimmy, didn't want to go, so Dad and I took off to investigate. At the station house, the clerk pushed a light crowbar under the grill. "Your delivery is on the platform," he said. "The crate can stay, but you must take the contents with you."

Outside, Dad pried at the crate. Suddenly it came apart, and out of it exploded a four-legged white burst of energy that nearly knocked us over as it streaked down the platform.

"It's a dog!" I shouted. Dad snatched the shipping tag on the crate and read the dog's name. "Victoria!" he shouted. Hearing her name, the dog skidded to a stop 50 feet away. "Victoria, come!" Dad called. Immediately the dog ran back to us.

She was a square-muzzled, lop-eared Llewellen setter about five hands tall. Her silky white coat flecked with charcoal glowed eerily in the harsh platform light. The sight of her made me gasp.

"Sit," Dad commanded. Instantly, she sat. "She's well trained," Dad said to me. "Tell her hello, Sheila."

At my first touch she erupted into an ecstasy of nuzzling, licking and yipping softly. Already I thought of her as mine.

When we got home Dad announced, "Look what we found at the station!" Victoria repeated the same enthusiastic greeting, but she got a different reception. Jimmy fled behind the couch. Mom looked reproachfully at Dad. "You didn't!"

"No I didn't," he responded. He showed Mom the address of the sender—a kennel in Virginia.

"Well she didn't ship herself," Mom said, retrieving Jimmy and lifting him up. He clung to her neck, hiding his face in her shoulder. I was glad Jimmy was afraid of Vickie because she was going to be my dog, not his. Almost eight, I knew I was wiser and more responsible.

Dad phoned the kennel owner. It turned out that my grandfather, before he'd died just a few weeks earlier, had bought Victoria to be trained as a bird dog. He'd never told us, but he had listed Dad as owner in case something happened to him.

After Dad explained all this, Mom took a deep breath and said, "Now, let's not get too fond of this dog. She's beautiful, but I have enough to do without caring for a large animal." My heart sank.

"Can't we just try her?" I begged.

"If she doesn't work out, I'm sure the kennel will take her back," Dad suggested.

"All right, we'll try her for one week."

Vickie had been observing the conversation. She wore a

worried, quizzical expression that seemed to say, "I know you're talking about me."

The next day we awoke to nearly a foot of snow. School was canceled, and after breakfast, Mom sent Jimmy and me outside with Vickie. We were happily building a snowman, when Vickie snatched Jimmy's blue wool stocking cap by its pom-pom and began prancing away. Jimmy gave chase, but Vickie stayed just out of reach. Soon Jimmy burst into tears and ran into the house.

I bit my lip. Mom wouldn't like this, and it was only the first day of Vickie's trial week. Vickie sat down, Jimmy's hat still dangling from her mouth. She cocked her head and looked at me questioningly, as if to ask, "Why would we leave when we were having so much fun?"

Moments later Mom appeared at the kitchen door with tearful Jimmy. "That's a *bad* dog taking Jimmy's hat," Mom said. Vickie drooped, her muzzle sinking down on her chest.

When Mom went back into the kitchen, Vickie bounded over and nuzzled against me, then nuzzled Jimmy too. She held no grudges.

I felt jealous. After all, *I* was the one who loved her. Jimmy didn't care a hoot for Vickie, I knew.

The week flew by. On Monday Mom had bought a large bag of dog food; enough, I thought, to last a month. I had taken that to be a good omen. Except for the hat incident, Vickie behaved beautifully. She never yowled, or begged or got in the way. However, by Friday the dog food bag was nearly finished, which gave me cause for concern. Vickie *did* eat a lot. Also, Mom seldom called Vickie by name and referred to her as "that dog."

On Saturday, "decision day," a huge moving van lumbered

by our house, stopping at the end of our cul-de-sac. Vickie took to running back and forth between our house and the van.

Returning from one of her sorties, she held an elegant woman's red leather pump in her mouth. With great ceremony, she deposited it at Mom's feet. I was afraid Mom would scold her. Instead, she said to Vickie, "Well, that's what you've been trained to do, isn't it?" Then she put the red shoe next to one foot and pointed to her other foot and said mischievously, "Go get the other shoe."

Moments later, Vickie was back with the shoe's mate. Mom clapped with delight and hugged Vickie. "Oh, what a good retriever you are! Finally you've had a chance to use what you learned."

"Does this mean I can keep her?" I ventured.

"I suppose so," Mom said, "but we'll all have to take care of her." Then she added, laughing, "And we *will* have to return these shoes."

Mom never complained about Vickie after that. She gave her a tattered hooked rug that became her bed in the kitchen. Whenever Mom sat in her favorite chair, Vickie invariably plopped alongside, her muzzle resting on Mom's foot. "I thought a gun dog was meant to sit at his *master's* feet," Dad teased. Mom laughed and said, "You don't feed her, Master."

As the months slipped by, Vickie continued to amaze us. She routinely fetched the daily paper for Dad. When we kids quarreled, she'd intervene by woofing at us. She led Mom straight to Jimmy when he got stuck in the marsh behind our house.

But it was on one June afternoon that Vickie proved her true devotion. Jimmy had gone to play with a neighbor child, I was swinging in a tree in the back yard, and Mom and Dad were working in our vegetable garden. Vickie was dozing in the sun.

Suddenly we heard screams, then saw Jimmy running toward us, his eyes filled with terror. He was followed by two snarling German shepherds. They had already nearly torn off one leg of his shorts. I froze.

Dad grabbed a shovel and raced to intercept the dogs. As Jimmy stumbled, the first dog was on him, snapping at his buttocks while the second dog jumped about barking fiercely. I screamed. Just then a white streak shot past Dad and catapulted into the fray—Vickie!

For a moment the shepherds let go of Jimmy and stood back. Then, baring their teeth and growling, the three dogs whirled about like a small tornado. Vickie, snipping and biting at the attackers, moved cautiously, always putting her body between them and Jimmy.

Suddenly one shepherd sprang away yelping, a red froth at its throat. Dad dropped his shovel and scooped Jimmy out of the melee. Vickie scrambled underneath the remaining shepherd and nipped at the loose fur of his dewlap. Finally, he catapulted off Vickie as if he'd been electrocuted. He loped away, rasping, his chest dark with blood.

Vickie did not give chase. She stood absolutely still, her tail switching slowly from side to side. She was trembling. I wanted to pet her, but, for the first time, I was afraid of her. Jimmy, however, was not. He wriggled free of Dad's grasp and ran to Vickie, throwing his arms around her neck. The dog nuzzled his face and licked his ear until Jimmy began to laugh.

There wasn't a mark on Vickie. Jimmy had a nasty gash on his rear end. The vet who treated the shepherds told us they had about 80 stitches between them. We never saw them leave their owner's property again. And, it seemed to me, Vickie never left Jimmy's side.

After a couple of days, this got to me. When I thought Mom was out of earshot I told Jimmy, "Vickie's my dog, you know. When we first got her, you wouldn't even go near her."

Jimmy looked at me defiantly and cried, "My dog too!"

"What's going on here?" Mom, who had been listening, demanded.

Tearfully I mumbled, "Jimmy's hogging Vickie."

"He loves Vickie, too, Sheila. Just as you do." Mom's gentle voice startled me. Normally when Jimmy and I quarreled, her tone was stern. "You don't have to compete for her love," she continued. "Vickie's love is big enough for all of us. Love isn't divided when it's shared. It grows larger."

Vickie had been with us for two years when, because of Dad's new job, we moved to New Jersey. Our small rental home sat right on a secondary highway. Unfamiliar with traffic and used to roaming free, Vickie seemed moody and listless confined to the tiny yard.

Then one day we heard the squeal of brakes, a thump and a heart-stopping high-pitched yelping. We ran out and found Vickie limping but alive. After that, even inside the house, she'd shiver when she heard cars whizzing by.

Three weeks passed, and Vickie was so dejected that she barely got up except to pace the kitchen at night. The vet said he'd never seen anything like it. "This dog has lost interest in living," he told us.

Mom and Dad decided Vickie's only chance would be back in our old, quiet neighborhood. When they told us, Jimmy and I broke down. "We have to do what's best for Vickie," Dad said.

He called a family that had always loved Vickie and had kept her when we'd gone on vacation. They said they'd take her.

The next Sunday we all piled into our station wagon. Vickie was in the back lying on her "bed." The two-hour ride was absolutely silent.

When we arrived at her new owners' house, they invited us in. Dad declined, explaining that we'd just like to say good-by to Vickie and go.

We all knelt down in front of her. Vickie came to each of us with that quizzical expression on her face, and we hugged her. Dad patted her flank, Mom caressed her ears and looked into her eyes. I threw my arms around her neck and squeezed her tight. Jimmy burst into sobs.

I finally took Jimmy's hand and led him back to the car. At that moment I felt closer to him than I ever had before.

Mom secured Jimmy in the front seat with Dad and got in the back beside me. Looking out the window, I could see Vickie, her tail swishing in farewell. I covered my face with my hands.

"Remember what I told you about love?" Mom asked. "That it only gets bigger when it's shared? Well now you're sharing Vickie with someone else who loves her."

"But it hurts," I said. I leaned against my mother and cried.

"That's the last lesson we all have to learn about love," Mom said. "After you learn to share, you learn to let go. Someday I'll have to let go of you. The biggest kind of love is doing what is best for someone else, even if it hurts. Do you understand?"

"Yes," I said because I was ten. I really didn't understand at all. All I understood was that she didn't let me go, not yet. She held me close all the way home.

from READER'S DIGEST

A Home for Gus

CRYSTAL WARD KENT

The first four to five years of Gus's life are a mystery. The little Jack Russell Terrier had lived on a farm for a time, and then was given to another family. They had him for only a year, then decided he was too wild. Gus's next stop was the animal shelter. It would either mean the start of a new life—and a real home—or it would be his final stop.

Gus was cute and perky, and shelter staff thought he could be easily placed. They featured his photo in a mailing, and soon visitors began seeking him out for adoption. A family with small children decided to take him home. They wanted a small dog, and the children thought he looked like "Wishbone," a popular children's TV character.

Unfortunately, the adoption was a disaster. Within two months, Gus was back at the shelter. The family complained that the dog was difficult to handle, aggressive, and could only be walked on a chain leash. He urinated in his bed and was too rambunctious, in short, Gus was not a suitable pet.

Back at the shelter, Gus began to wreak more havoc. Some volunteers did not want to walk him—he pulled aggressively on his leash, and growled fiercely as he wrestled with his nylon enemy. When the door to his pen was opened, he darted out, instigating a daily game of catch-me-if-you-can. He was very

vocal, barking constantly and some personnel were intimi-
dated by his noise. He was untrained and seemed untrainable.

Things were looking dark indeed, when Gus's guardian
angel appeared, in the form of a new staffer named Jennifer.
Jennifer was a dog trainer with experience with Jack Russell
Terriers; she had owned Jack Russells in the past, and had one
now. The shelter manager asked her to evaluate Gus. Could
this little dog become a good companion?

When Jennifer first saw Gus he was bouncing six feet
straight up in the air and the walls reverberated with his barking.

"I could hear him long before I saw him," she recalls. "Oh,
he had a lot to say! When I got closer, I could see this little ball
of brown and white fur just hurling itself up and down, like it
was on springs. I knew that Gus and I were about to have an
interesting relationship."

Jennifer knew that much of Gus's problem stemmed from
the fact that his previous owners had little knowledge of Jack
Russell Terriers. Jack Russell's are strong-willed, smart and
tenacious—like all terriers. They have a strong prey drive, like
to run, and need to burn off plenty of energy. They can be
hyper and vocal, and do best if they have some kind of job, or
other way to occupy their time.

Gus, like others of his breed, was small—about 20 pounds
and 15 inches tall—but he was all muscle. Despite his size, he
was quite capable of being more than a handful on a leash.

Jennifer realized that Gus's problem was two-fold. First, no
one had taken the time to train him. Second, because he was
difficult, he often didn't get walked or played with, that left him
with energy to burn and made him frustrated. The whole situation was a vicious circle—which she must break. Jennifer
knew that if she failed, Gus's chance for a happy home was

probably gone. He was six-years-old. He had three homes and been returned to the shelter once already. Younger, calmer dogs would be chosen before him, and his track record would put people off.

But Jennifer believed that somewhere inside Gus was a wonderful companion waiting to be discovered. She went to work.

First, Jennifer tested Gus for aggression. She was surprised to find that the "wild dog" was actually very gentle and easily let Jennifer pet him over his whole body. In fact, he lay down, rolled over and looked away—a canine sign of submission. As she spent time with him, she discovered that if anything, Gus was defensive-aggressive. He often pretended aggression because he was scared. He figured that if he acted fierce, that would scare off any threat and he wouldn't be hurt. Jennifer became convinced that somewhere in Gus's puppyhood, he had been badly frightened and possibly abused. He had never truly bonded with anyone. No one had loved him enough to win his trust.

Gus's urination problem also stemmed from fear. He urinated slightly when excited or frightened. If he could be given a sense of security, the urinating would stop.

Like many terriers, Gus was very intelligent, and full of play. He loved games, and he needed games to channel his abundant energy and challenge his active mind. Using a healthy mix of play and work, Jennifer quickly taught him basic commands. The little dog thrived on learning and quickly proved he was trainable. The leash problem was also resolved—if Jennifer ignored Gus's frantic tugging on the leash, he got bored and stopped. When his previous handlers had tugged back, trying to dominate Gus over the leash, the dog thought it was a tug-of-war game and responded with wild enthusiasm.

Gus's intelligence showed itself in his vocalizations. He had an extensive range of growls and barks, and much of his talk was just that—dog talk. He was not behaving fiercely, just communicating his many opinions the only way he knew how. As Gus began to have more play and activity, and a more structured day, his random, frantic barking lessened.

Jennifer decided Gus was ready for the final test—time in a home. She proposed having him spend a week with her. The shelter manager readily agreed, but there were other hurdles.

Jennifer already had a female Jack Russell Terrier at home. The aptly named Diva believed she ruled the roost, and so far, had never allowed any other dog to set foot on her turf, much less live there for a week. Jennifer decided to introduce the two dogs at the shelter, on neutral ground. If all went well, Gus would visit.

Amazingly, Diva and Gus hit it off, and Diva "consented" for Gus to come to her home. As the trio left, shelter staff winked at each other. They wondered if Gus would be back.

As the week passed, Jennifer was amazed at how well Gus fit in. He and Diva played non-stop; they shared toys and even Diva's dog bed. Gus was on his best behavior and obeyed commands to stay off furniture. There were no urination incidents. He was a wonderful companion.

Jennifer knew she didn't want to let Gus go. He was ready for adoption, but something had happened during their long work sessions together. He had become a friend. She loved the feisty little dog, and looking at him curled up happily with Diva, she thought "this is his family."

There was one problem. Jennifer was getting married in one week. When she broached possibly keeping Gus to her fiancé, he was adamant. No more dogs! Diva was enough.

"Dmitri said he was concerned about the upkeep of two dogs, the hair and all of that," recalls Jennifer. "But mostly, he felt left out. Diva was my dog—that was plain. Dmitri felt that Gus would be my dog, too, and he wanted his own dog, that he picked out. He never said any of this, but I sensed it—and evidently, Gus sensed it, too."

Jennifer finally coaxed Dmitri into at least meeting Gus and seeing how far he had come. The minute Dmitri sat down in the living room chair, Gus leaped into his lap, curled up and went to sleep. Dmitri was won over instantly. This was his dog after all!

The shelter staff were not surprised to hear that Jennifer wanted to adopt Gus. They happily presented him to her and Dmitri as a wedding present, knowing that the tough little terrier would live happily ever after in this home.

"He is so much a part of our family," says Jennifer. "He has his own toy box, and he and Diva are best buddies. He follows her lead on everything—good habits and bad, I'm afraid. And he is truly bonded now—for the first time in his life he has a family to love. He can't wait for my husband to get home. First thing, he's up in his lap wanting to be hugged. This was truly a match made in heaven."

Mighty Hercules

BARBARA BARTOCCI

One April Sunday, my children and I picnicked in the park. I was pouring lemonade when I heard a shout. Andy, my tow-headed eleven-year-old, ran toward us, holding what looked like a long, crooked stick. When the stick wriggled, the lemonade splashed across the picnic table.

"Mom!" Andy cried. "It's a garter snake. May I keep him? Please?"

My instinct was "No!" But the look in Andy's eyes made me hesitate. Andy was the youngest of my three children, and I worried about him. At four, he'd required surgery on his ears and subsequent speech therapy. A year later, his father died; the same year, doctors diagnosed attention deficit disorder. He had needed special schools in early grades and still required a tutor. And, like many ADD kids, he had grown up feeling "different" and "dumb," despite his very real intelligence.

From an early age, Andy possessed an affinity for animals. Growling dogs wagged their tails at his approach. Hissing cats purred. But dogs and cats were not allowed in our apartment complex. I looked from Andy's pleading eyes to the unblinking eyes of the snake. Its tongue flicked at me, and I shuddered.

"Where would you keep it?"

"In my aquarium. I'll put a lid on and never ever let it

bother you, Mom." He held the striped, black snake up to his face. "Please, Mom. Please?"

I'm still not sure why I said yes. But Hercules, as Andy triumphantly named him, came home with us.

Andy set to work at once, cleaning the twenty-gallon aquarium, lining it with rocks and dirt, setting a branch upright in one corner for Hercules to climb on, installing a light bulb for warmth.

I admired Andy's industry, and once Hercules was safely behind glass I could even admire the long, striped snake. In the sunlight, his scales danced and glittered, the way sunlight catches on a dragonfly's wing.

"He's not trying to sting you," said Andy, when I jerked back from Hercules' flicking tongue. "Snakes use their tongues to sense things around them."

To a boy with dyslexia, reading can be an excruciating task. Andy had never read for fun, even though his tutor told us he had overcome his early handicaps. But after Hercules' arrival, Andy checked out every book on snakes in the library. We were amazed at all he learned.

Even more amazing were the changes in Andy, especially after his sixth-grade teacher invited Hercules to school. Andy was smaller than most of his classmates, but I saw his shoulders straighten as he proudly carried the snake to school.

Hercules spent all spring in the classroom, under Andy's charge, and adapted well. Before long, Andy had only to stick his hand in the aquarium for Hercules to slither to his outstretched fingers and glide smoothly up his arm. On the playground, he looped gracefully around Andy's neck, basking in the warm Kansas sunshine, his tongue flicking Andy's cheek.

Hercules returned home when school ended, to be joined,

for Andy's birthday, by a pair of boa constrictors he named Mabel and Sam.

The boas were young, about eighteen inches long, and beautifully mottled in rich shades of brown and tan.

"How do you know they're male and female?" I asked.

"I just know," said Andy confidently. "I'm going to put myself through college by selling baby boas."

College! I marveled again at the changes the snakes had wrought. Here was Andy, who had thought he was "dumb," suddenly talking about college.

As summer veered toward autumn, Herc became Andy's near constant companion. Often, when Andy went out on his bicycle, Herc rode with him, sometimes wrapped around the handlebars, other times tucked into Andy's drawstring snake bag.

Seventh grade is a tough year for kids, and for shy, insecure Andy, starting junior high could have been a nightmare. But now there was a difference.

The lonely boy of a year ago smiled now. He held his head high and stepped confidently into the crowded school hall, knowing that the other kids whispered of him, "He's the guy with the snakes."

I remembered what Andy's teacher had told us on the last day of grade school: "Hercules has given Andy value in his own eyes. For the first time he has something no one else has— something others admire. That's a new feeling for Andy. A good feeling."

The snakes were a regular part of all of our lives now. When Hercules disappeared from the bathroom one day, after Andy had let him out to exercise, the whole family pitched in for the snake hunt. We found him in the closet, wrapped cozily around one of Andy's sneakers.

And we all watched, fascinated, when Hercules shed his skin, slithering out with a smooth, fluid motion to leave behind the old skin perfectly intact, while his new scales glowed with youth and promise. Carefully, Andy collected the old skin and placed it in the shoebox where he kept his valuables.

We never learned what sent Hercules into convulsions that spring. As far as we could tell, nothing had changed in his environment. But one Friday afternoon, Andy ran to me screaming, "Hurry! Something's wrong with Herc!"

Mabel and Sam lay quietly curled in their corner of the aquarium. But Hercules writhed and jumped. His tongue flailed the air wildly.

I grabbed my car keys while Andy wrestled Hercules into the snake bag.

Our veterinarian injected some cortisone, and it seemed to work. Gradually Hercules grew calmer.

Andy gently stroked his snake, and slowly Hercules reached up and flicked Andy's cheek with his tongue. He flowed again into a graceful loop around Andy's neck.

For several weeks thereafter, Hercules seemed fine. But then the convulsions returned, and we raced to the vet for another shot of cortisone. Once again, Hercules recovered.

But the third time was too much. Although the cortisone quieted the massive convulsion, it was apparent as we drove home that Hercules was dying. His long, lean body lay limp in Andy's lap. His scales, instead of catching the light, were clouded and gray.

He tried to lift his head as Andy stroked his back, but the effort was more than he could manage. His tongue flickered once, weakly, like a candle flame about to go out. And then he was still.

Tears rolled silently down Andy's cheeks. And mine.

It would be another year before Andy blossomed, seemingly overnight, into the six feet of linebacker's build that would carry him through high school. He went on to college, made good grades and, later, earned an M.B.A.

Andy never did raise baby boas, but Mabel and Sam stayed with us all through high school, bequeathed, at the end, to Andy's biology class. They never took the place of Hercules, though.

In Andy's top drawer, there is still a dried snakeskin. Before he left for college I suggested it might be time to throw it out.

Andy looked at me in horror. "Don't you dare!"

He touched the skin gently. "Ol' Herc . . . he was sure one splendid snake, wasn't he?"

Yes, he was. He gave a shy, lonely boy the first intimation of all he was—and all he could be.

from CHICKEN SOUP FOR THE CAT & DOG LOVER'S SOUL

LOVE IS UNDERSTANDING

"If you talk with the animals,
they will talk with you, and you
will know each other."

CHIEF DAN GEORGE

*H*ave you ever noticed that the animals in your family seem to understand the human members better than you do? They sense when someone is disappointed and trying to hide it. They can detect a hurt no matter how well we cover it up. They'll even cover up their own frailties so that we won't worry about them. Maybe it's because their love is so strong that they can see through the barriers we put up to protect ourselves.

Sometimes, though, it's the animals who need our understanding. They have problems, too. And if we follow their example and let our love lead us, we can help them.

Belle

TERESA TSIMMU MARTINO

The gray mare swung her body high in the air, and balanced on her back hooves. She reared above me where I had fallen in the dusty arena. I had been riding the mare, Belle, in the covered arena at Cormac Farm. Suddenly, she reared to her full height and came down bucking, lost her balance and fell. I was still struggling to rise when she leapt up from the ground.

Belle stood a moment above me. In her eyes I saw something hopeless and dangerous. Down she came, striking with both front feet, teeth bared. I had one moment to appreciate her shining coat and beautiful form, then survival took over my being. Rolling this way and that, I tried to get on my feet and yet stay out of the way of her pounding front hooves.

The *poof! poof! thump!* of the mare's hooves thudded in my ears. Time slowed into bright sparkling eternal seconds while I dodged her sharp hooves. My mind was strangely quiet. No thought, only instinct. Dust flew up in wide arcs in the afternoon sun. Something else was directing my limbs, saying faster than heartbeats, *This way, now that. Try to leap up and grab her head or run for the fence.* But Belle was working with that same power and wished for my life. I couldn't get up.

A small, silver-gray form wheeled between us furiously barking and snapping. The mare leapt back, surprised. Beanie, my dog, had managed to jump the arena fence to defend me. She leapt at the mare's face and snapped in anger. Beanie's bravery startled Belle, and that gave me a few crucial seconds to get on my feet.

After one desperate kick at Beanie, she finally galloped to the far end of the arena. Beanie and I sprinted for the gate and safety outside the fence. Beanie, proud of her achievement, stood panting, her scalp neatly cut with a wound five inches long. Fortunately, the kick had only grazed Beanie's head. Although covered in dust, I had escaped injury. Belle stood at the far end of the ring and snorted loudly to warn me. Belle was at war.

Life brings me creatures who are down on their luck. Wolves that have been chained in a basement. A horse that was isolated and starved. Abandoned wolves and horses headed for the meat market. I had ridden hundreds of horses in all stages of work and of many different personalities. By the time I met Belle, I had been a professional rider for about fifteen years.

One day in early spring, a slender, older woman named Elanor showed up at the barn. She was driving a truck and pulling a loaded horse trailer. She was English and her soft voice brought back memories of the gentle rolling hills of the country where I had trained.

Elanor shook my hand, and then took a deep breath. "I have a horse, a mare who is ruined," she explained. My eyebrows raised. She went on, "She was ruined by a man who beat her and isolated her and went so far as to starve her. I bought her out of pity, but. . . . " She looked me in the eye. "I've been told that the mare is unrideable. She threw the last trainer several times and he broke his hip. I want you to know that he felt that she should be destroyed. But I want to save this horse, I feel that people did this to her and that we should help her come back. I heard that you do this sometimes."

The last sentence hovered between a question and a statement. Elanor's face was kind and serious. She held my gaze and I thought a moment before I spoke.

"Some horses can be saved, some are very difficult. You realize that she may be insane from the treatment she has received. If she fought the last trainer and won, she has learned. It may be too late."

The horse whinnied plaintively in the rig. The woman smiled sadly, "It was your barn or I take her to the vet and have her humanely destroyed. You're my last hope." At this she put her hand on my arm. The sincerity of this gesture was frightening. The decision was now mine. Either I took the mare and tried, or the mare died. A hundred thoughts flew by.

It's dangerous, walk away.

You have two, beautiful, new colts to start. Think of them.

If you end up a cripple, you won't ride anything again.

Two assistants walked up, Beth and Drosk. They had heard the conversation. As they stood staring, I could feel their belief in me. I couldn't resist walking to the trailer to peer in at the stamping, sweating mare. "What's her name?" I asked. "Belle."

Her body was a dark gray, and her mane and tail a pure snowy white. She looked at me with white-ringed eyes filled with fear and hatred. It was clear that this mare detested human beings. But then, perhaps she had not met real horse people before. People who work with patience and compassion, whose hands can be trusted.

I accepted. The woman handed me a blank check to cover my expenses. Surprised, I stared at the check for a moment, but said nothing. We backed the rig up to an empty paddock. Belle was loose in the rig so we opened it up and she bolted into her new home. Then she stood and stared seriously.

Elanor looked at the mare sadly, turned, and gave me a soft, secret smile. She got into her truck and drove away. I took a closer look at the mare, who was a little more than fifteen hands high. Belle was mostly thoroughbred. She had a small short face, and big dark eyes under her snowy forelock. She was short in the back with big sloping quarters. When Belle turned, she looked like a bull fighter, quick and observant.

In the beginning, all we did was feed her. I spent extra time at her fence line watching. Belle didn't approach, but paced like a leopard. Then she would turn and stare in my direction.

In her eyes I saw danger for human kind. I know that criminal horses are very rare, and that 99 percent of the time they are created by the people who handle them. I know re-schooling abused horses and wolves can only be done with love. Firmness certainly, and no fear on the part of the trainer.

Could it be the same with human beings? There was a man who wrote me from prison. He described being in isolation and trying to keep the despair from his letters. But he was alone, utterly, and people on the outside feared him. I know this man had trouble when he went into prison, but now, after ten years in isolation, I wondered what this had done to his mind. Can humans be born as criminals? Or are they like the horses and wolves, responding to years of abuse.

After a month, Belle began to eat out of my hand. And three more weeks of my standing in her paddock patiently, she let me touch her. The joy that day brought! She shuffled towards me, and I felt her brush of soft muzzle. But after she ate the sweet grain, she wheeled away.

Two months later I began to feel confident that Belle's heart would mend. She let me brush her, and saddle and bridle her, though I had to watch. Belle would bite or kick if I wasn't careful. It was as if Belle was testing to see if I would beat her for bad behavior. But all I did was growl, and then she'd behave, but watch me carefully.

Then came the day I finally got on her. Belle stood still only a moment then bucked like a demon. She bucked so hard that my teeth rattled. She leapt up high and spun like a rodeo bull. I stayed on, fighting her urge to buck by trying to keep her head up and go forward. Belle was like the man in prison. She knew a lot about fighting.

An untouched horse, wild on the plains, is easy to train compared to a violent re-school that has experienced the wrath of humans. Over the years, these re-school horses have had to learn tricks in order to deal with abusive people. Belle knew many tricks; however, I managed to stay on till she was exhausted and stopped.

The next day I had my veterinarian look at Belle to make sure there was nothing physically wrong. Some horses buck because of back problems. Or they hold their breath when girthed up. Or they may have a hole in their diaphragm that causes them discomfort. But Belle was in good physical condition.

Day after day Belle bucked. We would both finish exhausted and sweat-drenched. My neck started feeling like I had whiplash. Belle grew angrier when she bucked. I merely stayed on and this became infuriating to Belle. She was used to another type of war. The war between enemies. The war between slave and master. But I fought her with the instincts of a lead mare. A struggle, but not with cruelty.

I hoped Belle would respect me because she couldn't buck me off, and in turn would realize that I respected her because I didn't whip her for bucking. . . .

Generally, a horse learns to buck. A horse started correctly will not buck at the rider's weight, no more than a pet dog would buck if the child she was raised with climbed on. Getting on a horse for the first time isn't the hard part of training; it's the years afterwards when the horse and rider learn to balance with skill enough to turn like a dancer.

In today's horse culture there are clinics that brag about starting a colt in a day, as if the quickness of it was the miracle. But old horse people know it takes years to create art. Horses as great masterpieces are not created in a day. An artist does not need to rush. With Belle I worked slowly.

In the old horse world, it was the apprentices' job to mount a horse for the first time, supervised by the master. This was because mounting for the first time was a simple thing to teach the horse. The master did the more difficult training that included the horse's ability to carry weight with the haunches and move under the rider with only a thought.

Belle had learned how to dump enough people to know a great deal about bucking. How was I to get her to stop? How could I teach her about the partnership between horse and rider?

. . . The next day I mounted Belle again and she started rearing. But this time, there was a new and frightening twist to her tactics. She would rear high and threaten, and then come down bucking. When Belle reared, it seemed as if she tried to lose her balance and fall. I began to despair and think that there was no way to reach her heart. Belle's owner, Elanor, did not visit the barn and she didn't call. She probably thought I was about to give up on Belle, who was one step from being destroyed.

A few nights later the coyotes who made their den by my house awoke me with their late night calls. Moonlight poured over my bed. I had dreamt.

In my dream, Pop and I were watching horses. The wild ones were jumping and leaping across the plains. They ran with the fierceness of fire and wind. Their aggression turned, by need, into the care of the herd. The lead mare, a gray with a long white tail, ran in front. Behind her were the other mares and foals, and in back, the stallion as black as pitch. The horses jumped everything in their way, creeks, ditches, and fallen trees.

Pop looked at me and said, "The way to reach Belle is by jumping her. Make her feel like a hero. The secret of life, Sister."

For a long time I lay in my bed and watched the yellow moon chase the horse clouds across the sky, jumping over the stars. I went back to sleep, thinking.

The next morning I built a low fence and lounged Belle over it. She devoured the challenge of the fence as if she were wild. Then she bucked and jumped with joy afterward.

After that, bit by bit, we jumped more and more. Something was shaking loose in Belle's heart. I could feel it crumbling under me when I rode her. Two weeks later I took Belle out to our cross country course and she jumped like a professional over the solid obstacles. After we completed the course, I praised her and patted her sweaty neck. Belle arched proudly. That was the first day she didn't buck.

From then on, when I showed up at the barn in the morning, Belle looked for me, and when I left, she called to me. Belle's aggression turned to affection, softened by the partnership of jumping that mimics the wild. In time, even Elanor could ride her.

. . . The last I heard of Belle was five years after she moved from my barn. Elanor was too old to ride her, so she gave Belle to a twelve-year-old girl. I saw them at a cross country event, running like the horses in my dream.

It was at that same event that I thought I saw a tall, handsome man with curly blue-black hair at the concessions stand. He turned and waved, and a moment later disappeared out towards the upper-level course.

from DANCER ON THE GRASS

Quite a Pair

RELDON BRAY

---

*M*om, who suffered from congestive heart failure and lived alone, was having another one of her rough days. While I sat with her at her house that afternoon I buried my head in the local newspaper rather than make her expend her energy talking. I turned to the classifieds, hoping to find something worthwhile in the dogs-for-sale section. I needed another dog to help me work the 80 head of cattle my wife, Rose, and I keep on our farm. My eyes flew right to the listing "Blue Heeler for Sale." Also called Australian cattle dogs, blue heelers are ideal ranch workers. They're born to herd, and they do it real well. Ann, the dog we had, was the same breed. I called the number in the ad.

I found out that Britches, a two-year-old, belonged to a boy whose parents had moved into town. Blue heelers need daily exercise and lots of space to run. Britches didn't have that anymore, so the boy's folks had decided to find a better home for the dog rather than coop him up. It was a tough but fair decision. I made arrangements to see the dog, then hung up.

"Sounds like an ideal mate for Ann," I said to Mom. I described Britches.

Mom nodded, then rasped haltingly, "It'll be hard for him to part with that boy, though." She paused to catch her breath. "You know how blue heelers can be one-person dogs."

I looked away. I hated seeing Mom struggle so hard to breathe. Despite the best of care and my constant prayers, each day she seemed a little weaker. Still, she remained cheerful, and I kept telling myself she'd get better soon. "Reldon," she spoke up, "the sooner that dog gets back to work, the better."

Seemed Mom always knew just what to say to me. Though I didn't get why she had to be so bad off, work was something I understood. I promised I'd go check Britches out that day.

When I saw the dog pacing around his little backyard, bluish head held high, I felt sorry for him trapped inside the fence. I made arrangements for the boy and his uncle to bring the dog to my place to see what he could do. The next day I watched Britches follow simple commands, cutting cattle from a small herd and guiding them into holding pens. I bought him on the spot.

After the boy and his uncle drove away, I gave Britches a pat on the head and called him to follow me. Instead, he plopped down on the ground, tucked his head close to his chest and refused to budge. I was barely able to get him to the house.

Eye contact is an important part of training a dog, but Britches refused to look directly at me. Nor would he follow a single command. "That dog doesn't even blink when I call his name," I complained to Mom.

"Poor fellow misses his boy," she said, then urged me to bring Britches to meet her.

"Up!" I commanded Britches that afternoon, trying to get him into the back of my pickup. But he refused to obey, even though I'd seen him follow the same order when given by his boy. Finally, I had to lift the dog onto the pickup's bed, then tie down his leash for fear he'd bolt. In Mom's driveway I unfastened the leash and commanded, "Britches, down!" He went through the plop, tuck, refuse-to-budge routine. I tugged gently on the leash, saying, "Come, Britches." No use. I pulled harder, but he resisted me with all his strength. "Who's training who here?" I snapped at the dog.

I almost had to drag him inside. Mom was sitting on the couch, looking pale and tired. "Come here, Britches," she said, stretching out her arms. He went right over. Her hands were shaking badly, but she still managed to scratch him behind his ears. "What a fine fellow you are!" she praised. Britches wagged his tail.

"I'll be darned," I said. "That dog won't even look at me."

"You just have to give him some time, Reldon."

"Well, I've never seen such a stubborn dog," I told her. "He's never going to accept me."

"That dog's got a lot of adjusting to do," she said. "Just keep working with him, Son. He'll come around."

Maybe she's right, I told myself. *After all, he does seem to respond to her.* I took Britches with me every day when I went to visit Mom. He'd run over to her when she greeted him, then stretch out in front of her, perking up to look right at her face every time she spoke. Still, the only thing he'd do for me was walk through Mom's front door. Mom was real tickled by my frustration, but kept assuring me the dog would come around.

I wondered about that. And I worried about Mom. She was getting so weak that she could only talk for short periods before needing a rest. One day in December I stopped in front of her spare room. Something struck me as different. Then I realized: This was the first holiday season the room hadn't been crammed with gifts and homemade treats for Mom's friends and family. Now it was too neat, too empty. I turned away quickly and went to fix Mom and me a simple lunch.

After I helped Mom to the table, we sat and bowed our heads. I thought about how many times we'd gone through this ritual together, how few times we might have left. I kept my head down longer than usual after Mom's breathless "Amen" so I wouldn't lose it when I looked at her again.

The rest of that day was quiet. We talked when Mom felt up to it, but mostly we just sat together. I answered the phone a few times. Always it was Mom's friends checking in. After one call I said, "You sure do have a lot of folks praying for you to get well, Mom." I forced a smile, then added, "Including me."

I had to lean close to hear her reply, which was barely a whisper. "Some things you can't change, Son. God doesn't always answer our prayers the way we think he should."

Driving home that day I couldn't get those words out of my head. I gripped the steering wheel so hard my fingers turned white. *She has to get better, she just has to.* After I parked, I sat in the truck, staring at the mountains. "Oh, Lord, help me," I prayed. "I know Mom's telling me she's not going to be here forever, but it's so hard to accept that. Help me come around."

Britches's barking from the truck's bed startled me. I went around to untie his leash. I reached over to scratch him on the head, but he retreated. It was the last straw. Pulling my hand away, I slumped against the truck and wiped my tears with my sleeve.

I had months' worth of unspoken sadness in me, and I don't know how long I stood there crying before I felt a gentle bump against my leg. Britches. He was looking right into my face. His tail wasn't wagging, and his ears lay low, but his eyes locked with mine. "We're quite a pair," I said to the dog. "You lost your master, and I'm losing my mom. What are we going to do?"

It was the first time I'd gotten a good look at his eyes. They seemed to me to be filled with misery and longing. *Is that the way I look to you, God?* I wondered. I stooped to stroke Britches's tense body. "You are without a doubt one of the finest dogs I have ever had the pleasure of meeting," I said softly. When I leaned my cheek against his silky head, he didn't pull away. "Good boy," I whispered. "I know how hard this change is, believe me," I told him. "I'm going to keep working with you. You'll come around." Britches relaxed, and for the first time in weeks, so did I.

Then his tail thumped against the ground. I felt a comforting warmth, despite the biting December wind. "Come on, boy." I headed toward the house. A few paces back, Britches followed.

The next morning I had to move some cattle down to the barn. I got Ann and decided I'd give Britches a shot at it too. At the truck I called, "Up!" and Ann hopped right in. Britches stood his ground. I was disappointed, but I tried not to show it. Instead I knelt beside him and said, "Britches, I know you know what 'up' means. Fine, you're still getting used to me. But from now on, we've got to help each other. Pretty soon you're going to be the finest working dog in the state of Arkansas." His tail thumped a bit more than it had the night before.

I stood. "C'mon, Britches, I know you can do this. Up!" He jumped into the bed of the truck.

By the time we reached the back pasture both dogs were leaning forward, bright-eyed and eager. I called, "Down!" and they leaped from the truck and raced toward the herd. They circled to get the cows moving, then weaved in and out to round up the stragglers. Britches zigzagged behind one headstrong cow, nipping at her heels, and I thought, *Mom was right. This is going to work out just fine.*

Mom died two months later. For a while I couldn't stand to be around people. By then Britches was always by my side. During the months that followed he was the only earthly comfort I had, and all the more so because of what Mom had said: "He'll come around." And whenever I watched Britches dash across a field to cut off a straggling cow, I found myself coming around too.

My Two Teenagers

SHARI SMYTH

$\mathcal{I}$ look at Roscoe sleeping sweetly in his crate, his paws twitching as he dreams. I wonder what a seven-week-old Labrador retriever pup dreams about. I envy him that his morning has been so peaceful while mine is shaping up as a minor nightmare. As it usually does these days, the trouble began with my 13-year-old son, Jonathan.

It started when I caught him dropping gobs of gooey hair gel on my antique mahogany table while using the mirror above it.

"If I've told you once, I've told you a thousand times . . . " I exploded. Once again we were bickering—me nagging and controlling, my son resentful and defiant. Hearing the whine of the school bus outside, I rudely pushed him out the door. I noticed Jonathan's thin shoulders sagging a little as he ran. *Good,* I thought, *maybe I've gotten through to him this time.*

Then later this morning came another call from the dean of students at my son's junior high school.

"Mrs. Smyth," he began hesitantly, "I know you've probably come to dread these reports as much as I do, but we've had another incident here you must be told about."

What now? I wondered helplessly. My mind raced over the catalog of recent transgressions Jonathan had committed. *He wasn't always like this.*

"In science class this morning," the dean said, clearing his throat, "Jonathan was carrying on and sprayed another boy's shirt with iodine. He must stay for detention and, of course, that shirt will have to be paid for."

My face burned with embarrassment and rage as I hung up the phone. The money Jonathan had been saving for new hockey gear would now go for the boy's shirt. That much I knew. But I was at a loss to understand what was happening to Jonathan, or what to do about it. Jonathan's adolescence had hit us like a tidal surge. When I wasn't quarreling with Jonathan, I was worrying about him, resenting this newfound obnoxiousness.

I try to shake off the morning's traumas and turn my attention back to the slumbering Roscoe. He has a public appearance to make. Roscoe is a Guiding Eyes puppy, and I have agreed to raise him until he's ready for formal guide dog training. I was warned by his breeders that he was the dominant pup of his litter and will be a real handful once he begins to assert himself. So far he has been a dream.

An hour later I am seated on a folding chair in front of an elementary school gymnasium filled with giggling, squirming children. They crane their heads for a peek at the sleek puppy on my lap. Roscoe's dark eyes casually scan his little fans. I glance at the grown-up guide dog sitting tall beside her blind owner next to me. "That is what you will be like when you grow up," I whisper into Roscoe's soft puppy ear. He steals a kiss and wags his tail.

We begin the program with Kathy from Guiding Eyes explaining my role as a puppy raiser. She tells the children that I will steer my dog from puppyhood through adolescence. I am to love and discipline him, teach him manners and basic commands and, when he is older, take him to public places such as restaurants and office buildings.

While Kathy talks, Roscoe chews his teething ring placidly. The children laugh at him because he has suddenly fallen asleep and is snoring loudly. Roscoe awakes with a start, bewildered, and cocks an ear.

I look out at their fresh-scrubbed faces. They seem so eager and cooperative, like Jonathan before he turned 13. There he is in my mind again. Jonathan. I am always brooding about what he used to be like or what I wish he would be like now. It's not so much what he does, but the belligerence he does it with. Yes, sometimes he is the same sweet kid I've always known. Usually he is. But other times he is moody, defiant. I hate the person I am becoming. I always seem to be carrying a grudge against my son, like today. I am anxious for him to come home from school so we can have it out about that boy's shirt.

Roscoe shifts in my lap and I snap back to the program. Audrey, the blind lady, is demonstrating how her dog, Eva, makes it possible for her to live virtually a normal life. The children are hushed with amazement. "Forward!" Audrey commands. Eva confidently leads her through a maze of chairs and around a grand piano. "Good girl!" There is a burst of applause. Roscoe sits up groggily and wags his tail. He believes the clapping is for him.

"No, Roscoe," I say softly. "Someday people will applaud you, but we have a long road ahead of us."

On the way home Roscoe whimpers in his crate. He is demanding to sit on my lap while I drive. This is not the Roscoe who came from the breeder a few days ago.

"No," I say firmly, keeping my eyes on the street.

The whimpering quickly escalates to a high-pitched yowl.

I slap the top of the crate with a loud whop. This behavior must be discouraged. Roscoe stops—temporarily. We battle all the way home and I begin to understand the breeder's warning. Roscoe is a strong-willed pup!

After lunch I can't find Roscoe. I call his name and whistle. Suddenly I hear a terrible racket in the next room and race toward it. Roscoe has cornered Sheba, our cat, who deftly springs to a table. "Roscoe, no!" I yell, joining the chase. Ignoring my command, Roscoe bounds after her, bouncing up and down from the floor. *Crash.* My beautiful African violets in their prized hand-painted vase splatter in a broken mess. Roscoe, the unrepentant, dives gleefully through the dirt, smearing it into the rug. I am appalled by his behavior: "Bad dog!" I shout.

His eyes gleam up at me triumphantly, challengingly. I think back to what the puppy manual advises about dominance. Be firm, it says, be patient. And always follow punishment with praise. Roscoe complies with my order to sit. Then I praise him to the skies. He is his old puppy self again.

I scoop him up and return him to his crate. Immediately he begins to whine; soon it is a full-blown tantrum. I need some peace, so I head off to the library. I won't be gone long. I want to be back when Jonathan gets home. I haven't forgotten what happened in science class.

When I return I hear Roscoe still carrying on upstairs. My temper is about to explode. It blows sky high when I reach the crate. Roscoe has completely torn apart his little domain. I yank him out of the crate, put him down on the floor and yell something I don't mean: "You will never ever make it as a guide dog! I don't want you anymore!"

This time Roscoe hangs his head in shame. His ears draw back and his tail droops. He is truly sorry. But I am still angry with his willfulness. He must learn to control himself. "You can't keep testing me like this," I complain. As I stomp away Roscoe follows meekly at my heels. He won't let me out of his sight. It strikes me that the little puppy needs me more now than ever. He seems to understand this somehow.

Suddenly a phrase from another manual comes to mind, the "manual" of love:

Love never gives up.

It is from First Corinthians 13, and it is just another way of saying that love always gives second chances. How many have I had from God? Too many to count!

Love does not keep a record of wrongs. Another line from First Corinthians. I stop and look out the window. In the distance I see the late school bus making its way up the street. I've been wrangling with Roscoe all day long, but deep in my heart I have also been wrangling with Jonathan, fighting the resentment that was left hanging in the air after our argument this morning, resentment I have not let go of. I *have* been keeping a record, a bitter record, of all of my son's wrongs.

Jonathan, I think, is trying to find his feet in life. It is a process we all go through, and it is not always pleasant. Strangely, in his search for independence, Jonathan needs me more than ever. He needs me to be firm yet patient, to help him find his way through a terribly difficult period. It is a learning process for us both, but he will never again be the little boy he was. He is growing up, and more than ever my love must give second chances.

I feel Roscoe leaning comfortably against my ankle. I look down and give him a rub on his head. "I'm sorry," I say. Something in his eyes reveals that he understands me, and he will try to do better.

A few minutes later the front door opens and closes. Jonathan stands in the doorway to the kitchen, tossing his gel-styled hair defiantly. He is braced for a lecture loaded with wrongs from his recent past. I surprise him, and myself. "Why did you do it?" I ask simply.

He studies me silently then sits down at the table and stares out the window. I strain to hear his answer.

"I don't know," he says, "I just wasn't thinking."

It is an honest answer, not an excuse. He shifts uncomfortably and volunteers that the right thing to do is pay for the shirt with his own money and write an apology.

Before he leaves I feel compelled to say something good about him. When I think about it, it is not hard. There are many, many good things about Jonathan. "Your dad and I appreciate how considerate you are about letting us know where you're going and when you're coming home."

Jon looks away in embarrassment and gets up to go to his room and study. As he leaves, I am full of love and pride for my son.

It is nighttime. Roscoe is asleep again, snoring in his little crate. Jon comes into the kitchen. He piddles around, then looks at me steadily. "Mom," he says, "I really am sorry."

"Me too," I gulp.

Quickly, before I can hug him, he's off to bed.

Dear Lord, I pray, *thank You for showing us how to wipe the slate clean.*

My Beloved Biddie

ROGER CARAS

Brigitte was a black toy poodle and was the third jewel in the crown, one of my three favorite dogs of all time. Now, there was a sense of humor! She was vain and she knew it and she laughed at herself. She could play the game with perfect abandon. She was with it, no other way can it be put, she realized full well how silly a place the world is and, well, she was with it. It was fine with her because she got everything she wanted out of life.

Once about every six weeks a very pleasant wisp of a young man, native of a soft and gentle place where the offal of the world smells like potpourri, I am sure, would manifest himself at our door and carry the unresisting Biddie away to his van, clutching her to his breast and cooing. Later that same day she would reappear, bathed, coiffed and all-over smartened. I never was able to deter the beautician from the fingernail polish and ribbon bit. No matter how intense my prohibitions, Brigitte would reappear as if both she and her beauty consultant had popped out from under a toadstool, she wearing a ribbon in her topknot that had been carefully color-coordinated with the fingernail polish chosen for that day and evident on all of her nails. I can't imagine what Biddie and the fair young man talked about while all of this was being done, but Biddie adored him and never minded going off in the van that led her to glory.

The important point is that Biddie thought it was uproariously funny. No matter which way you turned that evening, Biddie was posing, doing model turns, receiving the admiration of all. She jumped up on chairs when she heard anyone coming and stood there waiting to be examined and praised. When the adoration seemed to be flagging, she held out a paw and showed you her nails. She knew that was always good for a rise. She loved it, the little hussy—her behavior on the evening she came from the beauty parlor was markedly different from any other evening. She wallowed in praise and admiration and she damn well knew how silly it was. She was simply playing the game with the rest of us. Very often she was sent off to the parlor of her improvement when there was going to be a party or gathering of some sort that evening. With a house full of people available for her ego gratification the posturing became so intense she would sometimes have to be banished to a bedroom.

Biddie and I had a trick, a kind of parlor game. I would hypnotize her. It was like the old comic shtick where the comedian flops his head to the side as if falling instantly asleep. Biddie would sit on my lap with her little forepaws on my chest and I would start the routine:

"Brigitte Petite Noir," I would intone, *"look into my eyes. You are getting sleepy. You are falling asleep, your eyes are getting heavy. Now sleep until I awaken you."*

At that point Biddie would flop her head against my chest with her eyes closed. It really was very funny and as I look back I never felt silly doing it. It wasn't silly, really, it was a little bit of vaudeville in the parlor. It never failed to get approval from the crowd, whether they had seen it done before or not. As a matter of fact, scores of times the performances were done on request or command. I always feel good when I am interacting with a dog so I liked it, and Biddie simply adored it because she got attention. If the conversation went on too long without in some way involving her Biddie would jump up into my lap and assume the position. If I ignored her she did her part of the act without me. She would do it again and again until she got the focus of the room where she felt it should be. Again, there were times when she had to be banished.

Anyone who saw that little poodle and didn't think she had a sense of humor didn't have one themselves. It existed in her every posture, her every move, very nearly.

from A DOG IS LISTENING

Sunshine

NANCY B. GIBBS

Sunshine is a high-strung, boisterous cat who lives at our address. I didn't really want another cat, but when my daughter brought the rascal home, what could I say? He was so little, almost too little to be away from his Mama. He clung to me with his tiny claws and his "meow" was a high-pitched cry for help. His yellow-green eyes were filled with both mischief and love, so we couldn't help but adore him from the very beginning.

Even with a name as happy as Sunshine, he was mean! He was an attack cat, running throughout the house, jumping on the furniture, climbing the mini-blinds, and pouncing on every moving object. The veterinarian couldn't believe that we were able to live with him. She called him "the cat with an attitude." But we learned to avoid him and to run as we went through the living room. Not only did Sunshine bring joy to our home, he taught us the importance of exercise, sprinting in particular.

He loved the first Christmas in his new home, especially the decorated tree. He pulled it down three times during his first holiday season. I frequently came home from work and found him in the top of the tree along with the angels and ornaments, his eyes bright as the lights as he gazed down at me. Many times, Sunshine became a cat in flight. I learned to duck, as I sprinted faster through my living room.

When he was a year old, Sunshine came face to face with a truck. Even though he was hit, he was determined to get home. He dodged two other cars and crossed the street as I watched from my driveway. After extensive hip surgery, to the veterinarian's relief we brought Sunshine home. For some crazy cat reason, he decided to eat my pantyhose, so back to the vet's office we went. To her dismay, Sunshine was becoming one of her regulars. Six incisions and several hundred dollars later, Sunshine came home once again, meaner than ever.

Now Sunshine weighs in at a whopping twenty pounds. I have searched high and low for a cat dentist because his teeth are worse than his claws once were and his bite is definitely worse than his meow. He continues to be the boss of the house and keeps the entire household running.

For a few seconds every day, however, Sunshine is nice and accidentally purrs, while lighting our lives with love. Many times we tell him how lucky he is to be alive because nobody else in their right minds would put up with his challenging personality. He turns his nose up and lets out a domineering "meow."

That horrible day when Sunshine encountered the truck, I realized how much I loved him. I decided then that we will live together, teeth and all, for as long as he allows me to live at this address with him.

No Complaining

VAN VARNER

---

 oth my dog Clay and I are getting old and arthritic. In dog years, Clay's a lot older than I and maybe he's more arthritic too (at least I can still climb up on the bed without being boosted). No, my arthritis is the mild kind that moves around from my left hip to my fingers to the heel of my right foot with just enough pain to make me complain about it. And that's exactly what I was doing—complaining—to a friend of mine recently when she said, "Why can't you be more like your dog?"

I couldn't tell whether she was being serious or sarcastic—or both. "Meaning what?" I asked.

"Well, does Clay complain about *his* arthritis?"

I've been watching Clay lately and there's something to my friend's comment. On our long walks in the morning, Clay will trot ahead of me, his ears at half-alert, the soles of his paws flicking back like the hoofs of a race horse, his tail swinging pleasurably from side to side, when suddenly, without any warning, those old legs of his will give way and he'll go crashing down into the dirt, a startled look of noncomprehension in his eyes. I'll rush to help him but before I can get there, he'll be up again and back on the trail, the tail swinging pleasurably as though nothing had happened. No complaining. No feeling sorry for himself.

Come on, Van, take a tip from your old dog Clay. Stop complaining, get up, get on with the joyous business of living!

Aiming at Perfection

PHYLLIS HOBE

"No!" the trainer said. I stopped immediately and Kate sat crookedly at my side, biting playfully at the leash that dangled from my hand.

Mr. Magill scowled at us. Slowly he walked around us, pointed at my feet and Kate's paws. "They should be in a line," he said. "She's off to one side and three inches in front of you."

I thought he was a bit picky, and I guess he read my mind. "What we're after is perfection," he said. "Nothing less."

I flinched. Somehow I never thought of trying to train my dog perfectly!

"There's a reason," Mr. Magill explained. "It only takes one car to hit your dog. It only takes one moment, when you don't have control of Kate, for her to lose her life. Perfection in these exercises isn't for appearances—it's for your dog's safety. You've got to demand more of her—and of yourself."

That was all he said. That was all I needed to make me take our training more seriously. I took a step forward, said "Heel!" in a commanding voice, and Kate came lumbering to my side. "She's slouching," Mr. Magill commented. Obviously we had work to do.

I used to think God was asking too much of us when He said we should be perfect. But I'm beginning to understand what He meant. Perfection isn't for show. It's for our own well-being; it protects us from some of the sins in life. And it takes a lot of hard work.

"The Time Has Come"

FRED BAUER

When we got Duffy as a three-month-old pup, there were kids and lots of noise in the house. That was fifteen years ago. Now the kids had gone the way that kids go, the house was noticeably quieter, and Shirley and I were alone with our much-loved border collie, who was showing his age. First, it was arthritis that left him hobbling after our walks. Then his hearing and eyesight began to fade. Finally, he had kidney problems.

Amos Stults, who has been tending our animals for better than thirty of his eighty-five years, told us Duffy's days were getting short, but that with a special diet and tender loving care, he might be good for a few more months. And that proved to be the case.

Then one day after a business trip I came home to find him in bad shape. He had apparently suffered a stroke and could not get up to greet me with wagging tail and wet tongue. I phoned Shirley, who was visiting her mother in Florida, and reported Duffy's condition. She commiserated with me, then articulated what I had trouble saying: "The time has come."

"I wish you were here," I complained. "I don't want to do this alone." She made some understanding sounds before saying goodbye. I decided to wait until morning to make the decision.

"Could You take him tonight, Lord?" I prayed. Duffy's whining got me up several times during the night, and I knew he was suffering, but in the morning he was still alive. So I loaded him into the car and drove to the vet's office. There Amos and I put him on a gurney, and the white-haired vet turned away to prepare his needle.

"I love you, Duffy," I whispered, trying to hold back the tears. Then, as I petted his head and shoulder, something amazing happened: His shallow breathing stopped.

"Amos," I exclaimed, "I think he's gone!" The vet confirmed it. I had to smile. Either God had answered my prayers, or Duffy, sensing my agony, had done me one last favor. Maybe they conspired together.

A Visit With Sailor

BILL IRWIN

One day, a few months after I got my guide dog Orient from the Seeing Eye people, I paid a visit to the family with whom Orient's predecessor, my old friend Sailor (a shepherd, like Orient) had been placed after he was forced into early retirement due to back problems. Now that Sailor was secure in a new home, I wanted to say good-bye.

Sailor was glad to see me, and I felt a little bad bringing a new dog along. He certainly gave young Orient the once-over, and I could almost hear the question in Sailor's mind: *Why is this other dog wearing my harness?*

After dinner, while everyone was absorbed in a football game on TV and Orient was fast asleep in a corner, I felt Sailor sniffing around Orient's harness, which lay on the floor beside my hand. Finally I felt him slip his head into the center loop. No one would notice if we disappeared for a little while. "Come on, boy," I whispered, and we headed for the door.

Outside, Sailor jumped so quickly that he nearly pulled the leash from my hand. We started down the street in the cold air, and I felt Sailor come alive. Suddenly, he darted to the right to avoid a low-hanging branch that would have smacked me on the head. "Good boy! What a good boy you are!" I said, patting him.

We walked a couple of brisk miles together—our last miles. As Sailor led me along, I could sense him stepping proudly as if he were the most important dog in the world.

Finally, we came back to the house and paused on the porch. I slipped the harness off Sailor for the last time and bent down. I wrapped my arms tightly around him, burying my face in the thick furrows of his powerful neck and breathing in that full, wonderful dog smell. "Good-bye, old friend," I whispered.

Sailor had shown me a lesson. There was something virtually spiritual about Sailor's joyous submission to the harness. It was something I was beginning to learn about my own life, too. Through surrender, I find freedom and joy in living a life with God.

Elegy for Diamond

TRISH MAHARAM

I came to horses knowing only that my child loved them, and that because of her age much of the responsibility would fall to me. What I didn't know was that as a woman I would develop a love of horses that I'd never fostered as a young girl.

My six-year-old daughter had been passionate about horses since the age of two. In the park we'd come upon them and Hanae would call out from her stroller, her bike, her lanky growing body. Finally we sought out horses and ponies a year ago at the urban Overlake Farm just twenty minutes from home.

I left a note inquiring about riding lessons. Hanae and I knew this as the right spot to begin our horse adventure.

Just a week later the phone rang. "Trish, it's Gloria from Overlake Farm. I found the perfect pony. I was up in the Colville Flats rounding up cattle and we went into the slaughter pens."

I was listening but did not understand. I wanted to lease a pony, or just use one for infrequent lessons, but there was no room in Gloria's rhythm for questions and I didn't want to sound ignorant.

"This old mare, swayback and bony, came trotting toward me with her ears up high. I got as good a look as I could and she's just perfect for Hanae. It's better when they're old, they're gentler around children. But we have to move fast. She's bound for auction, then slaughter, in a week. I'm sure she'll cost next to nothing."

"I have to think about it," I heard myself say.

"Don't wait too long."

Gloria gave me the number of someone at the auction yards, someone who might know the mare's history, make it more palatable. I called, eager to hear anything that would persuade me to say "No."

"Well, John's not here and I can't be sure I know the mare. But you know, there's usually a good reason why they're here. If they were any good to anybody they'd have kept 'em."

I thought about the plants I'd rescued from friend's compost heaps. They were thriving in the garden.

I called Gloria. "I can do this. It'll be the perfect birthday surprise." But I wasn't really sure. This was my way, to leap into experiences, often with a surge of fear.

But by the time I drove with Hanae and my husband, David, to the farm the idea of a horse had already taken root. When we arrived I smiled at David, gave Hanae a firm hug and said, "We've gotten you your very own pony, a mare. We're all going to meet her for the first time."

Gloria was waving from a lower pasture. "Oh she's just the sweetest Appaloosa. You should have seen her trotting before. She's got a lot of spunk; must be twenty-five from the look of her teeth, maybe thirty. I heard this is your six-year birthday present." Hanae pulled back shyly. "Maybe we can get you on her back for a little ride today."

We approached the pony. She had a thick, gray-spotted, shaggy coat, a rug really, and she was big, more a horse than a pony. I rubbed her coat and mane shyly, feeling a layer of slippery grime cover my palm.

"She's loaded with lice powder. They're bound to get it in those slaughter pens. She and this mare over here." Gloria pointed to a thin brown horse with a quivering underlip. Her expression was deerlike. I thought hard about lice. I cringed but smiled.

The pasture was full of thistles and muddy earth. It felt cold and dank. My toes were already wet. This was unfamiliar territory. I suddenly realized this was not just the rescue of a pony—it was taking on responsibility for another living creature. She was ours and I knew absolutely nothing about horses. I looked toward David for consolation. He averted his gaze and looked somewhere far off. This was my project. He had clearly communicated that he did not want a large animal at this point in our lives.

We drove over every other day. An hour's visit would turn into three. Large bags of carrots were consumed over the winter by Diamond Feather, Hanae's chosen name for her pony. Minnie, another rescued horse, shared the shed. She was bony and meek, like a victim. Diamond stood beside her, an experienced matron, concentrating deeply on the chewing of her oats. They bonded with each other and whenever Hanae would ride bareback to the arena, Diamond and Minnie would neigh their good-byes loudly. It was always a woeful moment, that parting.

Often when we went to the farm I'd be sure that we could only remain for a certain stretch of time. But the sound of Minnie and Diamond's unified chewing was comforting, and errands or work paled beside the simple smell of horses and hay and the sound of rain on the shed roof.

By the time spring came along we'd been taught grooming. Jenny, Hanae's riding instructor, met with us once a week.

I sat in on the lessons, observing my daughter as she became tall and confident. I learned the methodical rubbing and lubricating of bridles, the brushing and currying, but there was a stiffness in my gestures. I moved around Diamond and the other horses with caution. My touch was distant, wary. I assumed they had a language I could not learn.

Diamond's left eye began to cloud over in the early spring and a series of vets dispensed ointments that I put into her eye once a day. Sometimes I'd let a day or two pass and often the ointment would coat more of the eyelash than inner eye. She was losing her patience with me. Her ears went back, which in horse language means "Clear out," but my ignorance kept me standing there. I'd rub her soft nose and kiss it until she lowered her head. This was the beginning of my knowing her.

No one properly diagnosed the eye, and it clouded over completely. We had to speak to Diamond when approaching from her blind side, touch her, so she knew our presence.

Gloria would come to us often, introduce us lovingly to the many other women who rode at the farm. Fifteen- and seventeen-year-olds, women in their forties, in their seventies. Comrades now. They would stop and chat about how well Diamond was looking. What I hadn't counted on was the deep sense of community. These women loved animals and it bonded us.

On a warm spring day Hanae ran ahead of me to the pasture. Diamond was down flat in the dirt. I sprinted toward her.

"Sharon," I called. She was grooming her horse. "Diamond Feather's down."

"Trish, it's all right, she's just sunning herself. I checked her already."

I still ran. It was the first time I'd ever seen a reclining horse. Minnie was quietly preening beside her. I sat cross-legged beside Diamond while Hanae collected bouquets of fresh grown grass for every horse within view. Diamond lifted her head and put it in my lap. It was a remarkable sight, the huge head settled on me and I rubbed her, stroked her, and wondered what her life had been before this. Had people loved her as I was loving her now? I brushed and curried her in spots that made her lips stretch far out and her teeth made silent nibbles; I felt then like we were becoming familiar with one another.

Gloria called one steamy summer day. "Trish, this is the perfect bath day. Come on over. Jenny's here and we've got Diamond grazing in wait."

I hung up. I'd been in the garden digging. There were ten plants waiting to get out of their cramped pots; Hanae was in her treehouse. But Gloria was on a mission. I laughed. Oh well. We grabbed some carrots and were off.

Diamond was already hooked up to Gloria's beauty parlor. She had a wild look in her eyes. Gloria had turned on her electric shears and the hair from Diamond's chin was dropping. I stroked her forehead and massaged around her temples, telling her it was all right. We were all with her, her congregation of women friends. We swept the hair away and hooked up the hose to warm water.

Her body stiffened at first and her head craned toward the sky. Gloria continued scrubbing and Diamond reluctantly relaxed.

"Oh, doesn't this feel good?" Gloria said, dragging the hose over Diamond's body. "I'll bet this is the first bath she's ever had." Words and water mingled. Dirt poured off her and Gloria chirped along. "There was an article in *Practical Horse* about a college girl with no money and a young man who was her trainer. They scoured the slaughter pens. The trainer was set on a big brown thoroughbred, but she was determined to have a little chestnut she'd spotted. She loved the face and the eyes on him. As of July he was the top First Year Green Working Hunter, which made him worth about six figures. There was a cover photo of them and the caption read something like, 'She had an "eye for an eye."' Of the fifty slaughter horses the trainer got at the pens he's only brought two back."

Summer melded into fall. We were visiting the farm every other day with lessons twice a week. I barely noticed the leaves changing because the air was still warm. Hanae had begun first grade and our visits to the farm were infrequent.

It was early November when we noticed that Diamond's right eye, her only good eye, was draining. Gloria thought it might be a plugged duct. I didn't think to call the vet. The next Saturday, Diamond's energy seemed low. Her eye was very cloudy. I knocked hard and fast on Gloria's door. Before I spoke, her words came. "I saw her eye, Trish. The vet's doing a group call this afternoon. She's great. I think you'll like her."

I had to wait for the vet. She was checking other horses. Horses were running in the pastures, basking in the warmth of the day. I wondered what would happen if Diamond went blind. I'd keep her and nurture her. They say you can still ride a blind horse. All their senses heighten. Diamond's winter coat was coming. I stroked it, remembering the hair she'd shed the previous spring. I massaged her forehead; my hands now knew her body, face, neck. She'd begun to rest her big head in the crook of my arm and close her eyes. I loved the smell of her: the combination of hay and mulching leaves and wind. All the elements clung to her.

"Sorry it's taken so long." My eyes opened, came back to

Diamond grazing. The vet had a firm spirited gait and her hair was silky red. She felt familiar.

"So this is Diamond Feather." Emily gently took Diamond's head in her hands and looked carefully at her eyes. "This looks like uveitis for sure. If you want to stop it where it is you have to be aggressive. I'd say six times a day with ointment for starters."

She gathered an ample bag of supplies, educating me about their purpose, while I stood dazed at the idea of six hours each day, the back and forth of it.

I looked at Diamond Feather. My posture was straightening, a sure sign of determination. Medicating a horse's eye can be a two-person job but I was sure I could do it alone. I roped off a part of Diamond's pasture for her and Minnie. I told her I needed her cooperation to make this eye better. She must have understood those first few days because she was very patient with my attempts. Gloria's daughter Linda showed me how to use a human twitch, a kind of nose pincher that focuses the pain on the nose so you can tend the eye, but I couldn't use it. I barely ever raised my voice with Diamond. It never occurred to me to be strict or severe with her.

I'd begin at 6:00 A.M., go home, get Hanae off to school, then again at 9:00, 1:00, 4:00, 7:00, and finally ten at night. Those first drives were arduous. I counted them off like a relay. Then I noticed that the weather was beautiful, the fall its most colorful in years. I urged myself to see the shapes as I drove along the lake. In the morning there was a mist like a snowfield, the schoolbus was picking up children. Hanae came infrequently. She was consumed with school and friends. This nurturing was tedious for her.

Often I turned the drive into a contemplation of the present, thinking about random significant questions: What is friendship? I'd ponder the mostly female relationships I maintained, those that gave and those that took away. It dawned on me how different it was to love an animal. There are no expectations in the giving. Not so with love of humans. There's a thread of need coiling through, a desire for something to be returned. I wondered if I could change this dynamic.

When I arrived at the pasture, Minnie and Diamond looked toward me. No false smiles, just a blasé acknowledgment. I felt a surge of love and friendship. They wanted carrots. Diamond put her head near mine. I breathed on her, found the bonyness of her face with my fingers. "I'm tired, Diamond, I want you to get better." She farted loud and long, pulled her head away, then gave it back. I had an immense love for this horse, this once mother. I wished she could tell me her story.

When I came home from the farm the phone was ringing. "Trish, it's Emily, the vet. I did some bloodwork yesterday on Diamond. It's not good news. It showed a high calcium count, which means a tumor or cancer. I'm sorry. You've given her such a good home. Maybe she's got a year. Sometimes these things snowball so you should watch her closely, her appetite, her bowel movements. We don't want her to be in pain. Go to three times a day with the ointment and keep in touch."

David and Hanae and I sat down that night. I explained that there was something growing inside Diamond Feather and we didn't know how long she'd be with us. We'd dealt with death—birds on our property, raccoons, fish. We'd created ceremonies for them, made little graves. But we'd never lost anyone we loved.

Hanae cried. It seemed effortful, like she thought she was supposed to. I held her and we conjured memories until bedtime.

Three days later I was headed for Diamond's last creaming at four o'clock. It was near dark on that gloomy day and I shone my headlights on the stable. Diamond was down and obviously in pain. She was rocking her body on the ground, her breath was heavy and fast. Minnie was sniffing her. It was obvious that she'd been down for hours. I drove quickly to Gloria's. The door was open but no one was home. I called the vet and left a note, hoping Gloria would arrive soon.

In the pasture I got down on the ground and stroked Diamond. I wondered if this was colic. There was a strong smell of ammonia. I threw my weight into her body, imagining I had the strength to lift her like I would my child. I cajoled her with words and kisses, and finally she rolled herself up and stood. We tromped around the little space to get some movement going inside her. I prayed for long loud farts but she just fell onto her front knees and lay panting. I made her a bed of fresh yellow straw like a wreath around her.

A woman I'd never met appeared, set up a lantern, and stood by me silently. Then Gloria drove up, bringing life and possibility to the solemn air.

Emily finally arrived. She was all action. Listening to the heartbeat. Me holding Diamond's head while Minnie looked over my shoulder; the steam rising in the ray of a flashlight.

"There's bad blockage and huge gas pockets. We've got to put her on a longe line and get her running." Emily tugged from the front, I pushed from the back, Robin opened the gate and we finally got her out of the muddy pasture onto the drive. Gloria ran after her with a rake. It seemed so inhumane, but the result would be her health. I took her halter and ran beside her, with her, all the time telling her she could do it. But she fell in a heap on the ground.

Emily faced me. "It's bad, Trish. This gas colic needs surgery and with her history I couldn't say if she could even make it through. She's in a lot of pain and there isn't another way to make this better."

I began to cry. "What are you saying?"

"We could keep her alive but she'd be in pain. In the past I've let illness go too long. It just doesn't seem right. My advice is to euthanize her."

I'd never had any experience making a decision like this. Diamond stood before me, big in the night, the steam from her body so alive. It wasn't until she fell again that I understood it might be her time. They all left me alone with her. I wanted Diamond to tell me, to give me some sign, but there was only the heavy sound of breath and a steady rain. What equipped me to make this decision? Only that I owned her. The concept of owning seemed ludicrous to me just then.

Gloria came to my side. "She's had a good year, Trish. Look how flared her nostrils are. She's trying too hard. There's a grave already dug up by Crystal. You can have it for Diamond. This way she'll be near us."

I thought of Hanae planting a bed of yellow and purple crocus and poeticus like slender fairies, and of Diamond Feather lying peaceful beneath them. She looked broken, her legs kicking on the gravel surface, and for one moment I felt sure, long enough to say, "It's time." The women gathered and we waited for Diamond to stand again.

It was a procession, a betrayal. It was the path we had taken so many times as Hanae rode bareback along the wooden path that led to the arena. As we turned and faced the hill heading away from her pasture Minnie neighed, and Diamond, weakened, stood in her familiar stance and neighed in return.

I could not promise Minnie that I would reunite them and their ritual tore at me. My whole body was sobbing. I remembered my mother saying that when we grieve it is for everything we have held or are holding. My sobs were open and unbarred like cats fighting in the night, or coyote cries and wolves howling.

At the top of the hill Diamond Feather fell, panting, and we urged her up, urged her to walk to her grave. There was an eerie light there, a kind of iridescence cast from the orange and yellow leaves. Gloria had to leave. In all the years of being a horsewoman she had never witnessed a horse being euthanized. I had to stay. I had to hold Diamond Feather so she would feel love.

Emily said it would only take about two minutes. Time felt hollow. I wanted to grip this moment, as though I weren't present enough. I didn't just want to observe her dying. I needed to be with her. A shot of blue liquid pierced through her neck and within moments her front knees thudded to the ground. I wished then that we'd waited until she'd come down by herself. I realized how controlled her other falls had been as her weight pounded the earth beneath us.

There are aftershocks in the muscles and the jaw and I rubbed the places I had massaged in the past until a silence settled over her body and all we could hear were the leaves falling upon one another. I kissed her temples for the last time.

Gloria was in the stable. She was crying as she told Minnie that Diamond was gone. I held Gloria close. It was the kind of hug that penetrates like a deep rain. Then I went home.

At dusk the next day we came as a family to say good-bye before Diamond was settled into her grave. Hanae had been very emotional and was angry with me because Diamond was her horse and she had not been present at her death. When we arrived, Diamond Feather lay undisturbed. Large colorful leaves had fallen on her body and neck. Her face was so tranquil, eyes closed, skin relaxed. She seemed already far away; only her body was left. We caressed her, my big hands beside Hanae's smaller ones. We let our hands rest finally on her eyes. Such a big gift she was.

from INTIMATE NATURE

Mission Accomplished

PAT WALDRON

"Maggie," our fourteen-year-old Yorkshire terrier, is six-and-a-half pounds of pure, unadulterated love covered with silky-soft black-and-tan hair. Maggie came to live with us when she was four years old, having been neglected and abused in her puppyhood. It would have been understandable if she had been sullen or fearful, but she was not. She was just filled with boundless love. From the first day she came into our home she immediately seemed to love and trust us, as well as the many friends who visited our home and all the strangers we met on our walks around the neighborhood.

In fact, there was so much love in this little ball of fur that we decided it wasn't fair to keep it all to ourselves. I thought that perhaps Maggie had a mission in life. She had brought so much joy into our home, maybe God had sent her to us in order to share that love and joy with people whose spirits needed some brightening.

So on a nice spring day Maggie and I went visiting at a local nursing home. In the recreation room, we found about fifty residents sitting around large round tables. Some were watching the news on television, some holding books or magazines they were not reading. Most were just sitting, waiting for something to happen. The room was very quiet.

Maggie and I made the rounds of the room. We stopped to talk for a little while at each table. I held Maggie close to each person so they could pet her if they wanted to. Most of them did, and many wanted to hold her on their laps. Some didn't want to let her go! Maggie wagged her little stump of a tail, wiggled all over, and loved them all. The room began to buzz with excitement. After we had covered the entire room, I promised to bring Maggie back. The residents were smiling. The room wasn't quiet anymore.

Leaving through the front entrance, I saw that a few residents had been taken outside to enjoy the sunshine and fresh air. With Maggie in my arms I stopped at each wheelchair for a moment to talk and let them pet Maggie. Then I noticed one last patient, whose chair had been pushed a little farther away from the others. She was propped up and strapped into the wheelchair, and sat unmoving with a vacant, faraway look in her eyes.

I hesitated just a moment, then bent over and asked her if she liked animals. A middle-aged man sitting nearby said, "My mother can't speak to you. She hasn't responded to anything in many months." But Maggie was already sniffing and nuzzling the lady's hand, so I lifted her hand and gently placed it on Maggie's soft back. The hand lay still, but slowly a beautiful, toothless smile spread over the lady's face, and the light of recognition began to glow in her eyes.

Her son's voice broke when he said, "Thank you. I thought I'd never see my mother smile again." My eyes were filled with tears, and I couldn't even answer. All I could do was give them both—mother and son—a hug. And one for Maggie, whose mission for the day was accomplished.

Treasured Memories

"All the animals I have ever known and
loved are with me always."

E. GEORGE HARDY

The hardest part of loving an animal is the realization that we can't keep them with us forever. Yet, in a way, we can, because God has blessed us with memories.

No matter how painful the loss of an animal, or how many times we have had to say goodbye, the animals we have loved will always be part of our lives. They have helped us to become the persons we are, and that's what keeps them close to us. As we live each day, they live it with us.

Ol' Spud

JAMES A. NELSON

I arrived home from school late one afternoon, and like most children, I was hungry. I headed for the kitchen to make myself a peanut-butter-and-jelly sandwich and a glass of milk, my usual snack while I read the *Chronicle,* our evening newspaper. Though I was only 8, I enjoyed reading the newspaper.

I said hi to Mom, who was tidying up the living room, then sprawled out in my favorite chair. I turned to the local news section and there, staring at me with doleful eyes from the holding pen at the humane society, was the cutest little terrier I had ever seen. His head was cocked quizzically to one side, a pose I found impossible to ignore. The picture's headline read, "I need a home."

Holding the paper, I strolled into the kitchen where Mom was preparing dinner. I always went to Mom first when I had an important request. Dad was often at work, and besides, Mom was always so positive. On top of that, she could work miracles with Dad when it came to getting a favorable answer to my requests. She took one look at my sheepish grin and said, "What have you got up your sleeve, Jimmy?"

I pulled the paper from behind my back. "Look on page five and tell me if that's not the cutest puppy you ever saw," I said.

The puppy looked at her with those sad eyes. Mom took the *Chronicle* and said, "Boy, does that pup know how to pose." I knew then my request was on solid ground.

"Now that I'm 8, could I have a pet?" I asked. "Every boy should have a dog." I had read that somewhere, and it sounded perfectly reasonable to me.

"Would you take responsibility for its care and feeding?" Mom asked. "I don't have time. He looks about 3 months old and will need a lot of training."

"You bet," I said excitedly. "You won't have to do a thing, just enjoy its company."

She grinned at my answer and said, "I'll talk to Dad when he gets home." Her reply made me warm inside because I knew this dog would soon be in our backyard, if he was still available.

When Dad came home later that evening, Mom approached him with outstretched arms and a smile. "Have you had a hard day at the office, dear?" she asked. Dad was an investment banker with a large brokerage firm and often came home "brain weary," as he put it.

Dad grunted, took off his coat and headed for his easy chair. I was standing in the hallway out of sight. "Here comes the question," I thought as Mom handed him a cup of coffee.

"You know, Jimmy is now 8 years old," she began, "and I think he should be taking on some grown-up responsibility. What do you think?"

"I couldn't agree with you more," said Dad in his gruffest voice.

Mom stood behind his chair, put her arms around his shoulders, and began turning the pages of the paper. She got to page five and said, "Isn't that the cutest puppy you ever saw?"

Dad squinted at the picture. "He is kind of cute, so what?" he said.

"Jimmy asked if we could go to the humane society and have a look at it. I think it's time for him to have a dog, don't you?" said Mom, who by this time was sitting on Dad's lap.

"I guess we could go down after dinner and see if it's still there," Dad said resignedly. He never had a chance.

After dinner we all jumped in the Hudson, our family car, and headed for the dog pound. As soon as we walked into the holding area, all the dogs started barking. They seemed to be saying, "Take me home. Take me home."

I spotted the dog from the newspaper right away. He was standing on his hind legs with his front paws against the wire mesh. Mom and Dad took one look at him and said to me, "What are you going to name it Jimmy?"

By this time the dog was wiggling in every direction. I was sure he would turn himself inside out. His dark brown color reminded me of a freshly dug Irish potato, and I liked potatoes. "I'm going to call him Spud," I said gleefully, "because that's what he looks like—a potato, all round and brown."

After filling out the necessary papers, we headed for the Hudson. Spud, of course, was on his best behavior. He rode quietly, snuggled in my lap, all the way home.

After we got home, I made Spud a nice bed from old blankets down near the furnace in the basement. While he got acquainted with Mom and Dad, I ran all the way to the store for dog food. I had seen many ads featuring Friskies dog food. Since Spud looked like the dog on the label, it seemed like the logical choice. He ate Friskies the rest of his life.

Spud's adoption was the beginning of many exciting times in my life. He was never far from my side. Mom called him my shadow. I loved the winters with him best of all. He was not only a great snowball catcher but also a dandy foot warmer. Each morning Dad built a fire in the furnace. From his bed in the basement, Spud could hear him coming; as soon as Dad opened the basement door, Spud bolted up the stairs to my bedroom. Hearing his tiny feet on the hardwood floor, I ducked down under the covers, anticipating his arrival. Spud jumped onto my bed and worked his way under the covers to my feet. Occasionally he licked them with his warm tongue, causing me to laugh. Then both of us would snooze for another half-hour before I had to get up.

When it was warm, I could hardly wait to get home from school to take Spud to a nearby park. We often played fetch until dinnertime. More often than not, we were late for dinner. Mom would scold me but couldn't help laughing as Spud would try to get her to take the ball he laid at her feet. She just couldn't stay mad at Spud, or me, for very long.

The nearby woods also held adventure for us. Spud enjoyed chasing squirrels and anything else that moved, including butterflies. He never caught anything, and I'm sure he wouldn't have known what to do if he had—he didn't have a mean bone in his body. The only unnerving encounter we had happened when he came upon a porcupine and decided to investigate it with his nose. As you can imagine, a trip to the veterinarian was necessary. I was told by Dad, "Jimmy, don't you ever let this happen again to Spud, or I'll have to show you just how sharp one of those quills can be." Even though I knew he was joking, I took the lesson to heart and stayed more alert on future adventures. Ol' Spud never got tangled up with a porcupine again.

Over the years, Spud taught me responsibility and brought

me great enjoyment with his loving companionship. He was a friend to the whole family. Mom often said, "He's so much company for me during the day, Jimmy, that I want to feed him tonight." More than once I caught Dad stroking Spud's head and saying, "You're not good for much, you old pot hound, but you'll do until something better comes along." Spud would look up at him with his soft, dark eyes and smile, or so it seemed to me, then shiver slightly with pleasure.

Spud and I were companions all through my youth, up until the time I was drafted into the army. I vividly remember asking about Spud in my first letters home. Mom replied that since I had left, they let him sleep in my room instead of the basement. "He seems much happier there than anywhere else," she wrote.

In my 12th week of advanced infantry training, I got a letter from Dad. As I walked back to my tent after mail call, I wondered why Dad would write. He had never sent me a letter before. I cautiously opened the envelope and read, "Jimmy, Spud died last week, we all are sorry. He got into some poisoned meat someone in the area had put out, and the vet couldn't save him." I felt like someone had kicked me in the stomach. I had lost an old friend.

When it was time for my first leave, two months later, I was sad that Spud wouldn't be home to greet me. But Mom took care of this situation in her usual, surprising fashion.

When I arrived at my house, there on the porch, wagging its tail, was the second-cutest little brown terrier I had ever seen. Mom, standing off to the side with a smile on her face, said, "We already named him Jimmy—Spud."

I'm 66 years old now. I live in a modest apartment and have no pets. My ex-wife and I had four children, and as they were growing up, we acquired a variety of animals. Yet when I close my eyes and try to think of all these former pets, the one that comes to mind first and matters the most is the dog staring at me with doleful eyes from the pages of the newspaper, Ol' Spud.

from DOG & KENNEL

The Quail Chorus

EARL HAMNER

*O*nce more I longed for the sound of bobwhite quail. Even though we could afford a larger house in a "better" location, we didn't want to leave Avocado Drive. The only thing it lacked as far as I was concerned was the call of the bobwhite quail.

I found an advertisement in a magazine. It was in the back pages where the print is small and where you find ads for compost makers (six tons of recycled garden waste for pennies!) or your life's story put to rhyme for only two dollars. A company in Georgia was offering a "Quail Kit." It included an incubator, twelve fertile bobwhite quail eggs, and a book of instructions. I sent for it.

When the kit arrived, following the directions, I arranged the twelve eggs on the metal grid inside the oval plastic see-through lid, connected it to an electrical outlet and hovered over it. My quail chicks were due to hatch in twenty-one days.

Word that "Earl Hamner is hatching eggs" got around the neighborhood. The younger people on the road were enchanted and would drop by every afternoon after school for a progress report. Some of the older people began looking at me with the same stare Jane's uncle gave me when he found me immersing my hand in the Mississippi River. I didn't care. I had long since become the neighborhood eccentric and it didn't matter what anybody thought of me at this point.

When after thirty days nothing happened, I assumed that nothing would. I cracked one of the eggs, suspecting it was rotten. Inside I found a perfectly formed baby quail, dead and dehydrated. I looked for the egg-beak on its forehead with which it was supposed to have cracked open the egg and released itself. It was there, but had never been put to work. I suspected that I had not provided the proper amount of moisture to the eggs. For that reason the shells remained hard and unyielding, even with the special cutting beak they had developed.

I was discouraged, but determined to try again. This time I bought a professional incubator and set it up on my writing desk directly behind my typewriter where I could keep an eye on it.

For the eggs, I returned to my friend in the west San Fernando Valley who owned the game bird farm. She was still wearing her cap that advertised Alfred Hitchcock's *The Birds* and she recognized me right away.

"You got yourself famous since the last time you were here," she said by way of greeting.

"I didn't realize I was that famous," I said.

"You're that one on *The Waltons*," she said. "The first time I heard it, I recognized your voice. Are all them stories true?"

I explained that some were and some were not, but that most of them had a genesis in some event in my life or the experiences of my family.

"I'm crazy about that Grandpa," she said.

"He's a lovable man," I replied.

"Is he married?"

"I'm afraid so."

"That's a shame," she said. "I could give that man a run for his money."

Once she learned that Will Geer was unavailable, she lost all interest in *The Waltons*.

"How is that rooster I sold you, and the two little hens?" she asked.

I filled her in on the adventures her chickens and I had been having, and she agreed that I had failed in my first attempt by not providing sufficient moisture to the eggs. She sold me twenty-four quail eggs and suggested that if Will Geer's marital status were ever to change, she would appreciate knowing it.

This time I set up my incubator with special care, turning each egg once a day, and keeping a watch on the water level, which I had learned was of the utmost importance. And believing that a watched egg never hatches, I stopped hovering and went back to work.

I was at the *Falcon Crest* production office when Jane called and said, "You had better get home if you want to see your quail being born." And then she added, "All the other kids in the neighborhood are already here."

Jane's reference to the other kids did not go unnoticed. I had long known that I was considered a peer by every ten-year-old on the street. This came about in part, I think, from the fact that I am a kite fancier. In the days when we had the great open field across from our house, I was there almost every weekend when there was wind, flying one of the kites from my collection.

To this day I have not lived down the fact that a kid named Jeffrey Van Zanten came to the door and asked Jane, "Can Mr. Hamner come out and play?"

At any rate, I arrived home to find that all the other kids in the neighborhood were indeed gathered in my study where they were watching the birth of my quail.

They were in different stages of being hatched. The birth would begin when an egg would give an almost imperceptible quiver. Next the egg would rock ever so slightly. What was causing the movement was the tiny creature inside attempting to saw its way out of the egg shell with its egg tooth.

Once it had sawed a sufficient distance to open the egg, the damp little chick would take a deep breath and expand itself so that the shell would split in two. After an hour or two of hard labor, the tiny thing would lurch about until it had disengaged itself from the shell.

Sympathetic "oh's" and "ah's" would go up from the audience as each quail infant struggled to enter the world.

The effort would exhaust the little bird so that once the egg had split, it would lie there recovering its strength for its next move.

My friend at the bird farm had advised me to prepare some shredded hard-boiled egg yolks for the infants' first meal, so while the newly born chicks were resting up from the trauma of entering the world, I began boiling eggs.

As soon as they could struggle to their feet, they began searching for food and once I placed the egg yolk in the incubator they began to feed.

"Good show, Mr. Hamner," said Jeffrey Van Zanten when the last egg had hatched. I thanked him and then sent all the human youngsters home so that the new arrivals could rest and get acclimated.

Within days their pinfeathers had developed. Within a week they learned to eat a special mash I had bought in addition to the hard-boiled egg yolk. Scott and Caroline helped me with the feeding, but Scott balked at giving them egg yolk.

Because they had so recently been egg yolks themselves, he felt it smacked of cannibalism.

From the day they were hatched, I stood by their pen and made the bobwhite call. It seemed to me that they listened. One or two of them would stop in their heedless running around and cock their heads as if something had attracted their attention.

Within about four weeks, they were large enough to be transferred to the elaborate pen I had built for them in the garden house. The pen was about ten feet long and was enclosed with chicken wire. I had built perches and runs, and planted patches of grass and arranged a bird bath for them, and done everything I could to make it a natural habitat. The quail seemed appreciative and at home.

Every night when I arrived home from my office, I began whistling the bobwhite call to them, but there was no answer. And then when they were about three months old I drove up to the garage, parked and began calling to my quail. Did I imagine it or did I hear a faint call reminiscent of bobwhite?

I went to their pen and they came to the wire to greet me, for they had learned to associate me with food. I tried their call, but this time there was no answer. Perhaps they were too interested in the food I had delivered.

Some days later when I drove up in my car and got out, there was a single bird call from the direction of the pen. My heart did a somersault! I had brought Virginia to California. I had re-created a golden moment from my childhood. I had called and my quail had answered me!

Within a week I had only to drive up and stop my car engine to be greeted with a chorus of bobwhites. And by the time I came to their cage, they were waiting to be fed.

They were about four months old when I decided the time had come to release them in the field across from our house. Catching them and transferring them to a cat carrier was no problem because they had lost any fear they might ever have had. When I reached the spot where I planned to release them, I sat beside the cat carrier for a while to allow them to become acclimated. After fifteen minutes or so I opened the door of the container. At first, one little fellow ventured out, and others followed casually. They seemed perfectly at home scratching in the grass for seed and small insects.

When I decided to withdraw, I stood up and quietly began to walk away. The quail continued feeding until one of them spotted me leaving—and came running after me. His action alerted the other birds and they followed until I was being trailed by a procession of twenty-four young quail, all in a straight line, one behind the other in tandem, following me as if I were their mother!

I tried just once to shoo them back into the field, but when they looked to me in confusion I did not have the heart to turn them out into the world. It was just as well, for in minutes every cat in the neighborhood had assembled and were eyeing my bird-children hungrily. There was even a red-tailed hawk that had spotted them and was circling overhead.

And I knew that after dark the keen noses of the coyotes would smell them out and they would all be gone by the next day.

I brought them all back to their pen where they were safe. For many years they continued to recognize the sound of my car and would welcome me home.

from THE AVOCADO DRIVE ZOO

Miracle Foal

GAYLE BUNNEY

I do not know of anything more special than a newborn animal. The mewling of a nest full of newborn kittens. Puppies, not yet completely dry, lined up at their mother's breasts, suckling contentedly. The baby calf, so new in this world, already bouncing around his mother, getting the feel of the earth beneath his feet. Most of all, the newborn foal, peeking out from behind his dam, eyes big and bright as his first glimpses of things yet to come.

Over the years, there have been so many foals in my life that I feel truly blessed to have been there over and over again to welcome them into this world. Each and every one of them holds a special place in my heart. I only have to close my eyes and I can picture them all over again, their warm fuzzy noses, their impossibly long, gangly legs, and their soft, new hides, every colour in the book, waiting to be rubbed and stroked by a kind hand.

Some hold an even more special place in my heart, for they are the ones who touched me with their will to survive, or perhaps had to overcome a poor start in life.

At an early spring horse sale, I purchased a brown and white pinto mare heavy in foal. She was so thin: except for the bulge of her belly, she was little more than hide and hair stretched over a rack of bones. She was only at my place two days when she gave birth. The newborn filly foal was not only slightly premature, but because her mother did not receive enough feed to nurture her foal properly in her womb, the filly was the smallest I had ever seen born from a mare that size. She lay on her bed of straw, every bone in her tiny body outlined beneath her skin. Her legs could not have been much bigger around than a man's middle finger. As weak as a kitten, she could not stand on her own and needed her first meal badly if she was to survive. I propped her up into a sitting position, and then boosted her to her feet. Matchstick legs trembling, she fought to stay on her feet. When she had some balance to her, I nudged her to her mother's side. Clumsily, she sought the teat that could give her strength through its nourishment. Weak as she was, she still managed to grab hold and suck for all she was worth. Once satisfied, she collapsed in a heap and soon dozed off. Every two hours, those first couple of days, I was at her side, helping her up and pointing her in the right direction. I named her Miracle, and marvelled at her strong will to survive. She was soon bucking and playing around her mother, like a mischievous child, seeing how far she could push her mother's patience. Her fine coat of hair, almost cream and white at birth, soon darkened into a brown and white pattern, like the mare's. By weaning time in the autumn, she was practically as big and sturdy as the other foals, except her hair, which still remained as soft as silk. When someone bought her, I felt an emptiness inside like I had lost my own child, having truly been touched by a miracle.

from HORSE STORIES

My First Horse

TERESA TSIMMU MARTINO

The sun is coming back after the short days of winter. Now is the time when the horses start losing hair. As they stand in the pasture, long tufts float on the brittle breeze and come down to rest on sharp, gray-frosted grass. Their horses' blooming coats are a bouquet of color. Bay, dun, black, chestnut, rust, dapple-gray.

Stallions, mares, geldings, and foals—the family of horse. Stars on faces, pearly socks on legs, whorls in hair—all are signs of wisdom or luck. Special horses carry birthmarks on their necks or shoulders, like thumb prints. My father, Pop, pointed out these marks to me when I was only four years old. With a hushed voice that hinted of mystery, of sacred things, Pop whispered, "The horses are blessed, chosen by God."

I met my first horse when I could barely walk. At two years old, I stumbled into a pasture, drawn to the wonder of the tall, yellow stallion. He stood patiently as I gripped his legs in my hands, and pulled myself upright. That was my first gift from a horse—support. Later, my relieved parents found me, and it was no surprise to them that my life turned into a career with the four-legged spirits that grace the grass.

For thirty-five years now I have watched the horses with passion. Horses are my family, sisters, and brothers. They are also my teachers and medicine people that walk my fields. With their mystery and magic, the horses have taught me the speech that transcends verbal language, they have shown me spirit and family and leadership. Pop once said, "You want to know what is around you? Ask the horses."

The horses have left tracks deep in humanity's consciousness. They run in people's blood, bred into them like spirals of DNA. This love of horses will keep a horse person from buying food for herself in order that her horses are fed. And the sweat of horses and the drumming of their feet gather horse lovers together as a tribe.

Horses are the demi-gods who gave us power. Their leaping strength, along with alert eyes and swift muscles, allowed humans to be four-legged and run on the plains and carry our spirits. And now, through the grace of horses, I can go back to the time that my Native ancestors spoke of—when the animals could speak. Back to a time when the horse and human molded into one, whether the mythic Greek centaur or the Native warrior and pony.

Pop taught me to care for my horses before I care for myself. He said they would always honor me through their work if I did this. He was right. For all of my adult working life, the horses have fed me and kept me free.

On this particular spring morning light offered hope for the damp and dark Pacific Northwest. But still, the chill cut through my blue-leather chaps and my toes were numb in boots with clinging frozen mud. My students worked patiently, learning the level of commitment needed for caring for the horses. They were acolytes as they scrubbed water buckets, cleaned stalls, groomed and fed horses, and rubbed leather with oil and waxy soap.

The horses knew they were special. Their patient faces were comfortable as they watched us move about busily tending to their needs. They looked at us with sweet sympathy, but they knew they deserved this care. The horses were fed before we ate. Their comfort came before ours.

This much I know is true. Horse people are like the little trotting sheep dogs who are bred for years to care for the lambs, or the children in India who give feed to the sacred cattle. This is the way it has been done since the beginning of the partnership between horses and humans. We are happy when working horses, ignoring cold and mud and danger. This is our life, there is no other. The horses know this and they watch us carefully.

The paradox of horses is that they do not *have* to carry us, but they agree to do so. "Why?" I asked one of my students, tall and thin like a colt herself. Then I answered my own question. The horses give their consent and bring a grounding that humanity craves. The horses carry the power of wildness that graciously allows us to fly above the land.

The true relationship with horses is like cells in the body. Cells came together to form a body. This is true of all the land and all life but with horses especially, because people who love horses can ride them and the two can become one.

My assistant, Summer, held the colt's head loosely as I stood next to the young horse and leaned into him to tell him with my body what was coming next. Summer was seventeen, the same age I was when I turned professional. "Work with your body," I told Summer. "Listen with it. Your body will tell you if the colt is ready for the next step." The colt stood calmly, listening to my voice, watching me with soft accepting eyes, feeling my trust of him through my body. Summer continued to hold his head lightly as I talked. "You will feel it in your stomach if it is wrong. The colt sets the pace for learning. He'll tell your body." Summer nodded sagely.

The colt had never been ridden. He and I were starting something that has been done ever since someone watched the wild herds thunder across plains and imagination. I have worked with more than seven hundred horses over my career and this was the forty-third colt that I've started. The colt gave me his consent and stood quietly, ready for me to get on him. I have never had a colt buck when I've gotten on. Always, I have asked, and they have given me their consent.

I held up my good leg, the other one weak from repeated injuries. Summer caught it and legged me up the colt's brown shoulder to his warm, bare back. As I stretched across the colt, I wondered, *Who is training whom?*

Did humans really domesticate the horses or did we just form a partnership? Cooperation is how all life survives. Domestication is a generational process that works both ways. I believe the horses gentled and tamed humans as well. Humans were once the great hunters of horses but now we serve horses as if they were our own kind, members of our family. Civilization would be different if it were not for our partnership with horses.

Feeling the warm body of the three-year-old colt, I imagined how the relationship between horse and human began. We have been together for at least five thousand years. Early humans dreamed of horses and painted their images on cave walls in flickering light.

Perhaps someone got an idea and thought: *Maybe it would be possible to become horse-like by getting on its back.* I imagined that someone found an orphan foal. Or maybe hunters killed a mare with a foal and then saw their own human children reflected in the foal's eyes. And in the mare's blood they saw their own fate. Early humans understood that the land gives generously but also takes back. Hunters knew that one day they would lie as still as their prey. The ancestors felt a responsibility for the foal and made a commitment, a promise to it. Then maybe some child playing with the baby horse climbed on its back and called out to Mom and Dad, "Look! Look!"

Once the horse and human accepted and trusted one another enough to ride together, the human became as swift as the elk and had the senses of an antelope. Suddenly, distances opened up for humanity. They could pursue game like a lion or a wolf. The horses allowed us to become a four-legged animal, a spiritual and bodily transformation into the creature that we admired.

Perhaps something about being human with our rational thought and our anguish at the impermanence of life, left us lonely. Humanity needed companions with better senses and no long thoughts that dwelt on death. The old people told me that the horse and dog, our partners, came in from the wild to share our lives and ease our fears.

Tradition is a big thing for horse people. And students inherit their teachers' traditions. The classical traditions were only written down a couple of hundred years ago. Most knowledge has been passed down from generation to generation, from teacher to student. My students inherit from me generations of horse work, knowledge gleaned carefully since the beginning of the partnership.

Often my thoughts drift back to *my* teacher, Pop, and the

first horses that lead me down this life path. A herd of weaned pony foals stood in a field of dandelions and lupines and sunshine. Pop, tall and bronze skinned, carried me through the gate of a rustic post-and-rail fence. He set me down among the tall flowers and curious foals. Placed among the ponies at four years old was momentous for me. It was my initiation.

"You pick out one for your own, Teresa," Pop said. I searched the faces that surrounded me in a loose semi-circle of warm earth colors. One pony was smaller than the rest. A sturdy little gray with a saucy face and warm wise eyes. She walked up and nuzzled my hand, sniffed my hair, considered taking a taste of me, then being a mannered pony, decided against it. Placing my hand on her neck, I said, "This one, Pop!" That was my first real horse.

The gray pony became a confidant, a patriot, and a companion. I named her Babe and called her B.B. for short. Pop always called her Rusty because she was the color of a rusty gray nail held in sunlight. Babe was only six months old, too young to ride, so we spent our time together in the fields. Babe grazed close beside me, while I stared up at the clouds and listened to her tear at the grass. When Pop came home from work he would help me brush her, and show Babe how to tie and lead and pick up her feet. Teaching Babe to carry me was easy. I would get on her back when she was laying down and she would groan and sigh, but lay there quietly while my child hands clutched at her mane.

Pop didn't really let me work Babe until she was three years old, and I was seven. By then, I could ride Babe into the golden hills and shady orchards near my home. My mother would weave my long dark hair in twin braids down my back, then I would pull on old jeans and boots, and join Babe in the fields.

What did we do, Babe and I? What all horses and children have done. Nothing and everything. Time slowed, disappeared while we watched clouds and chased our shadows through tall grass whipped back and forth like sea water. At any given moment Babe's head could jerk up, her ears prick, and nostrils widen. *What is it?* Babe's body asked me. *Brown's dog or a neighbor girl on her restive thin, bay mare?* Together we would watch and wait. Babe gave me the sharp senses that I would later expand in adulthood, and perfect when I hunted with Mckenzie the wolf.

On the hill above our white house, there was a little sign that pointed and read, "A. Martino." Whenever Babe and I would trot by that old white sign, I believed it meant that there was only one family like mine. My father's first name was Andrew. Perhaps that is why now, as an adult, I go by "T. Martino."

For fun I would put up little obstacles for the pony and ride her bareback at a full gallop down the steepest hills, my arms outstretched, shouting, "Watch me Pop! Watch me!" At a young age I learned that on horseback the world changes. Suddenly you can gallop, you can fly. Horse senses melt up to your soul, absorbed through skin and legs pressed tight.

Perhaps some people think that riding horses is cruel and that my poor pony, Babe, was dumb and shy, and had to put up with me, her master. Oh! But that is not the way it was. For those who move in close to horses, so close that they feel the horses' soft breath, they know that horses love, need, and want a good partnership. They look for it even in humanity.

Poor Babe wasn't fast. The neighbors' horses could always outrun us in the honor-bound races we held in the tall old orchards. Other friends' horses were bigger and faster, but Babe could jump, climb the steepest trails, and was unafraid of fierce dogs. She let me do all of these things with her without saddle or bridle, and only with her little halter that Pop had made.

Babe was not a pushover though. One time I tried to lead her through a broken fence line and she refused. For more than an hour I pulled on her, coaxed her—anything—but she would not move. Finally, I had to give up and go around. But on the other hand, Babe actually let me dress her up. One time I put ribbons around her feet and one of Pop's shirts on her. God knows whose pants. Her patience was saintly in that respect.

Falling off Babe became a skill I learned over time. She never bucked but I slipped off and collected my share of bruises, cuts, and tears. After a fall, Babe would nose me, concerned, waiting for me to get back on so we could be on our way. When I fell, Babe would never leave me. I long for the days when Babe would wait for me to get up. It was good to have a loved one wait for me after I had fallen. But I learned, like life, I must remount!

As Babe and I grew older, Pop taught me how to sit on her back, balanced, and how to use my weight to talk horse language. This is the empathic speech that runs along muscle and skin, the listening look of pricked ears that reads sights like a dictionary and feels thoughts like a psychic. Horse language is not merely telepathic but rather it is as if all bodies were connected and thoughts ran between them.

Pop taught me to put these feelings and emotions into my mind, and my body would interpret them, and then the feelings would run along my muscles and be communicated to the horse. By learning to put my conscious mind in every part of my body, rather than just in my head, I could talk with a horse in incredible ways. Now, my talk with horses allows me to ask difficult things from them, like jumping cross country, or being ridden for the first time, or creating intricate dances. Constantly, I test my communication. If it is correct, the horse does what I ask without force.

My days with my first horse still live in my body. The warm sunlight, the dusty spicy smells of summer, the glimmer of lake water dancing, and my bare feet buried deep in Babe's soft, long belly fur. Her head down in knee-high grass, with me on her back, Babe and I shared a horse's life. Step . . . graze . . . chew, chew. . . . Swish the flies. . . . Step . . . graze . . . chew, chew. The Greeks saw centaurs, but I know what they really witnessed—the *partnership*.

from DANCER ON THE GRASS

Turning Mourning Into Joy

ELEANOR SASS

As a single woman living by myself in a small Manhattan apartment, I was sometimes lonely. But I never intended to get a dog until the day that Dick, a friend and colleague, asked me to take care of his dachshund Gertrude while the family went on a vacation. I did, and enjoyed every minute of it. So later, when Gertrude had puppies, Dick and his wife Betty offered me one and I said, "Yes." That's how Heidi came into my life.

Eighteen years later, she left it.

I tried telling myself that I was fortunate to have had her companionship for so long. But it didn't help. I missed her dreadfully. Well-meaning friends reminded me that she'd been failing—her eyesight was poor, her hearing gone. I didn't care. I wanted her back.

One day while sitting alone in my too-quiet apartment, I found myself calling her name. "Heidi . . . Heidi . . . " tears streaming down my face. Then, in a moment of silence, a still small voice seemed to answer, "I'm here."

Instinctively I knew it wasn't Heidi. But my crying stopped and a calmness settled over me. I got up and went to the window. As I gazed up into a clear blue sky, the words of Jeremiah came to mind. Though my call wasn't to God, I knew He'd heard. And He understood. It was the beginning of my healing.

During my mother's lifetime, I'd often rely on her to take care of Heidi when I could not. Before leaving on a trip I'd tuck Heidi into her traveling bag and off we'd go on a forty-five minute subway ride from Manhattan to my mother's house in Queens. There I knew she'd be safe and happy until my return.

After my mother died in 1983, good friends came to my aid, volunteering to have Heidi stay at their homes. But while I was very grateful, somehow it wasn't the same. I longed for the reassurance and comfort my mother had always offered.

With Heidi gone, the days were long. Then one night I had a dream. In the dream, I could see Heidi sitting contentedly in my mother's lap. So reassuring was this dream that I sat up in bed, turned on the light and reached for my Bible. "I will not leave you comfortless," I read. "I will come to you" (John 14:18). God seemed to be telling me that Mother was still taking care of Heidi, and He would take care of me.

Confident that all would be well, I turned out the light and went back to sleep.

After a while my friends began asking me when I'd get another dog. "Never!" was my reply. I had gotten through the terrible pain of losing Heidi. I didn't want to suffer that way again.

One afternoon an ASPCA van was parked in front of the building where I work. A sign indicated that, inside, dogs were available for adoption. "Why don't we just take a look?" a coworker suggested. Reluctantly, I agreed.

All of the dogs available were medium-large or large size. "Definitely not right for my small apartment," I said with a sigh of relief.

Another day a veterinarian telephoned. "I have a nice pug that needs a good home," he said. "Why don't you come to see him?" I did go to see him, but when the pug was brought to me he paid absolutely no attention to my offer of a pat. *That's it,* I thought, *I'm not supposed to get another dog.*

Sometime later I went to Maryland to visit a friend whom I've known since high school, Nancy Bamford. She introduced me to her family's latest addition, a long-haired dachshund named Casey. Throughout the weekend Casey would often jump up into my lap and gaze at me with his soulful eyes, as if he were trying to tell me something. And each morning when I opened my bedroom door, there he'd be, waiting. At the end of my visit Nancy mentioned that she was planning to breed Casey. She wondered if I'd like to have a puppy.

My mind drifted back eighteen years to the day when I got Heidi. Suddenly I knew I couldn't pretend any longer: *I really did want another companion.*

Yes, I thought, *it will be a female, and I'll call her Sassy.*

Is there a pattern and a purpose in all this? I'm convinced there is. I know God sent Heidi to me because He knew that I was lonely and desperately needed the love and companionship that she gave me in such abundance for so many years. Now I'm sure that just as Heidi was perfect for me, so this little creature, not yet born, will be perfect for me, too. That's how God works in human lives. That's why He promised to turn mourning into joy.

I know He will keep His promise.

My Friend Mollie

MARION BOND WEST

$\mathcal{T}$he instant my husband walked toward me I knew something was terribly wrong. I'd been away all day at a seminar. It was now late afternoon.

"Mollie's hurt bad," Jerry said simply and quickly. I think I let out a low moan. Then I began asking questions. Early in the morning, just after I left, our beloved four-year-old collie had been hit by a car and seriously hurt.

In my mind I saw it happening. I didn't want to watch, but I couldn't stop the vivid pictures. Jerry had stayed home from work on a Friday to catch up on yard work and to be with our 13-year-old twin sons while I was at the meeting. Thoughts of *if only I hadn't gone* began. I tried to force them away.

Mollie hurt. I couldn't yet believe it. Memories of the first time I saw her eased into my racing mind. It was sweet relief from the horrible pictures of her darting out in front of the car.

After our 17-year-old mutt Muff had to be put to sleep with disorders of old age, we didn't talk about dogs much, even though we are dog people. Then one fall I mentioned to Jerry in a casual way that I'd been thinking about getting another dog. A collie. I suggested it almost hesitantly, knowing what loving another dog would involve. I almost hoped he'd say no. He beamed, "I've been thinking the same thing. A collie for

Christmas." We searched the want ads that day and then drove out to see some collie pups. There were four left. Jerry picked up the best looking one. While he held it, a smaller and more timid puppy came up to him and laid her head on his foot. She didn't make a sound. He put down the frisky pup and picked up the shy one. She laid her head on his shoulder, glancing once at him briefly. "The other dog is finer," my husband announced weakly.

"I know," I stroked the long-nosed puppy, "but he's not for us, is he? This one is." When we learned the puppy's mother had Love as her middle name, we named our choice "For the Love of Mollie." The people we bought her from kept her until Christmas Eve so she could be a surprise for Jon and Jeremy and our teenage girls, Julie and Jennifer.

When I saw Mollie again it was Christmas Eve and Jerry was bringing her into the kitchen with a big bow around her neck. She seemed afraid and unsure of our love and acceptance, but uncomplaining—hopeful. I was afraid and unsure too that night. Our 17-year-old daughter Julie had just become engaged. I knew I had to give her up. Perhaps that's why I clung to Mollie with such deep needs. From the beginning I loved the dog far too much. Eventually our entire family did.

She grew into a majestic beauty, but even more beautiful was her spirit. Content in our large backyard, her world, she never wanted to venture out without permission. She fancied herself a guardian to those she loved. Often she tried to impress us and make us believe she'd chased off some terrible enemy. She barked at airplanes and turned around joyfully for our approval when she saw that she had "driven" the planes away. We always praised her. After a bath, she would run like a race dog around and around the yard, then tumble into one of

us. During the hot Georgia summers, one of the boys filled up
our yellow wheelbarrow with water, and Mollie immediately
hopped in and dunked her head. She could hold her breath for
a long time and would look up at us from beneath the water
with a comical expression on her face.

Gentle beyond all comprehension, she romped with our
cats and chased them, only to let them escape. One of her favorite sleeping spots was the back steps. When I opened the door
to allow the cats to come in or out, they simply walked over
Mollie as though she were a huge sable-and-white door mat.
She would raise her head and look with approval. If one of the
cats wanted in on cold nights, Mollie learned to throw herself
against the door and open it, allowing the cat to enter. But she
would not come in herself until someone said, "Okay." Then
she would bound in and down into the den as though it had
been months since she'd seen us. Before she went back out
she usually ate the cats' food while the cats watched, seeming
almost to approve.

We often took her on family walks through the woods.
How she loved it, charging ahead of us, then circling back to
check on us. I suppose my favorite times with her were early in
the morning. I would go outside before seven and sit on the
back step in my nightgown. She would come up and lay her
head in my lap the way she did the first time she saw Jerry. The
world smelled wonderful and new and moist. I would tell her,
"I love you, Mollie Sunshine." She would look right into my
eyes and wag her magnificent tail. I know she understood. And
her love was always totally unconditional and never changing.

She had no fear of cars. She assumed that everything that
moved loved her as we did. Her only fears seemed to be thunder and the garbage man. She barked at him each week, look-

ing over her shoulder at me as if telling me that she would protect us.

It had happened so suddenly. Jerry had been cutting the front grass and had let her out to walk alongside him. He took his eyes off her for an instant, and she darted into the street. She'd done it before, but there was so little traffic on our street. This time, she picked the wrong minute to investigate something on the other side of the road. We were critical of people who let their animals roam. We rescued stray dogs from the highway. How could this have happened to our Mollie, right in front of our house?

My husband said she didn't cry out or struggle as he ran to her. She appeared relaxed, almost apologetic as he took her to the vet, five minutes away. X-rays revealed a badly fractured hip and pelvis and a broken tail. Her tail would have to be removed during surgery. It was broken where it joined her body.

"Well, why aren't they operating now?" I questioned.

"We have to wait until Monday to see if her bowels and bladder are working. The vet said he has to know that before surgery can be done. He has an orthopedic vet ready to do the surgery Monday morning."

"When can I see her?"

"Tomorrow. They're closed now."

Thoughts of Mollie alone at the clinic tormented me. I phoned around until I located the vet and asked him countless questions. I didn't really listen to his answers. I wanted him to assure me she would be fine. He didn't. He told me that I could see her early in the morning. I didn't sleep well. I prayed that Mollie was sleeping comfortably in her cage. When I slept, I dreamed she was running through our backyard again—without her tail—but nevertheless running, barking at planes, guarding us.

The next morning we waited for the clinic to open. Suddenly the vet was bringing Mollie to us. She looked alert. The vet brought her outside to see if she'd go to the bathroom in the grass. Jerry and I fell to our knees and put our arms around her. We talked to her and asked her questions. I suppose vets get used to people like us. She sat erect, looking almost normal. She watched a plane overhead, but did not bark. "I love you, Mollie Sunshine," I whispered.

The vet assured us, "She's not in pain. I've never seen a dog so broken up in so little discomfort."

"Well, we have been praying and asking God not to let her hurt."

The vet nodded. "That's it then. Try to keep her moving," he said over his shoulder as he went back inside to the busy clinic. For over two hours we hoped Mollie would go to the bathroom. Nothing happened. Finally the vet suggested we take her home for the weekend. Perhaps, at home, she would relieve herself in her own backyard.

At home Jerry took her to her beloved backyard—her world. He laid her in a favorite spot—under a large oak tree. The cats, Joshua and Jessica, came over to rub against her. She gobbled up everything I gave her to eat. I didn't bother with dog food. She got steak, hamburger, roast beef. As it became hotter and the gnats and flies bothered her, we brought her into the cool den by the fireplace, another of her favorite spots. She looked perfectly normal lying there, as though she might bound up the steps any minute.

Surely by tomorrow she would relieve herself and we could go ahead with plans for the surgery. It was going to be an expensive operation. We decided to cancel our upcoming vacation in order to have the money for the surgery and then to be at home with Mollie and take care of her.

By Saturday night she still hadn't gone to the bathroom. She would lick her paws and groom herself after eating. She couldn't reach her hind part, so it began to look a bit rumpled. I would brush it, and she would appear in good shape again. Our married daughter Julie came by to see her. Julie had worked for the vet who was treating Mollie. Mollie lifted her head high as she recognized Julie bending over her. Since she couldn't wag her tail, she sort of gave Julie a smile. Julie knelt for a long time and didn't say anything. "Looks good, doesn't she?" I asked hopefully.

Still looking at Mollie, Julie answered softly, "No, Mama. She's putting on a brave, wonderful front for you. See how tired her eyes are. It will be highly unusual if she comes through this. I've seen this type of injury before." Julie got up and walked upstairs without looking back. After Julie and her husband left, I went back into the den. Mollie put her head in my lap. She sighed and looked deep into my eyes. She wasn't smiling. My tears came suddenly and unexpectedly, and deep agony exploded inside me like a volcano. My tears spilled onto Mollie's face so that she blinked her eyes. Jerry came and sat by me. We didn't say anything. We just held Mollie and made terrible noises crying.

Sunday morning we got up and went immediately to the den. Mollie was unmoved, like a statue. I decided that I simply could not leave her and go to church that morning. The rest of the family stayed home too.

On Monday morning Jerry gathered Mollie in his arms and put her back under the oak tree. She looked perfectly content. A plane flew overhead, and she looked up. One of the cats came over and lay by her in the grass. I began to pray that

Mollie would give up. I couldn't watch her try so hard any-more. Jerry came in, and we stood at the kitchen window. "Why won't she give up? Lay her head down and stop that ridiculous smiling," I said. "What in the world does she have to smile about?"

We were running out of time. I phoned the vet and told him we were bringing Mollie in. I drove, and Jerry got in the backseat, holding Mollie. She laid her head back on his shoul-der like a child, and I wondered if Jerry might be remembering the first time he brought her home on Christmas Eve. Looking at passing cars as I drove, I saw that none of them contained dogs. Suddenly I envied people who didn't allow themselves to love a dog in such a ridiculous fashion. Why were we dog people anyway? Why couldn't we love rocks or butterflies?

In a few moments we were in the familiar examination room. Mollie was on the sterile, steel table, which she didn't like. The vet came in and said, "Hey, Mollie." He examined her and then in a direct manner for which I will always be grateful, he said, "She has absolutely no control over her bladder or bowels. They are totally destroyed. If we operate, you will have to give her an enema daily and she will have chronic kidney in-fections and endless pain. She will require constant attention. You really have no choice."

I heard myself say, "No!"

The vet said quietly to Jerry, "You will need to sign some papers."

I heard my husband say, "Of course." I was grateful for his courage and quick action. They left the room, and Mollie and I were alone, my hand on her. She was half sitting up, looking directly into my eyes. All my emotions seemed frozen. I knew they would thaw out at home, but I was grateful that for now

I stood like a mannequin. No feelings. No movement. No thoughts. No words. When the vet came back in the room, I moved toward the door to leave. *Don't look back,* I told myself. *Don't you dare look back.*

I looked back. Mollie and I stared at each other. I knew she wanted to wag her tail because that impossible smile crossed her face. Not understanding how it was possible, I walked mechanically out of the room.

At home, Jerry and I still had Mollie's fur clinging to us. We brushed ourselves off. The clothes didn't matter. It was our hearts and spirits that needed help.

Jerry changed into office clothes, kissed me and left for work. I didn't manage my usual "Have a good day." In my heart I just wanted him to get through it. The children were off playing; our daughter at work. They had taken it much better than Jerry or I. I was almost angry with them for being able to handle it, when I couldn't.

I was alone, standing at the kitchen window, wanting to look out into the backyard, but afraid to. *This is ridiculous. I can't be afraid of my own backyard. I have to live here.* But I knew I was afraid. I couldn't make myself walk out into a yard without Mollie. I flung myself on the sofa in the den and stared at the ceiling. My emotions were alive again. I cried out, calling Mollie's name over and over. *I'm some kind of a nut,* I thought as I sobbed. I couldn't get myself together. I had to have some kind of relief. The grief that held me in a vise seemed to be cutting off my breath, as though I were being held under water.

Then I remembered in Psalms (34:18) it said that the Lord is close to the brokenhearted. "God," I called out, as though He were up in the kitchen, "please come to me. It doesn't matter that it's just a dog. My heart is broken. You promised to be close to me. You promised! Please come and start a healing process in me. I need You."

Almost instantly my grief shifted into another gear. A lower one. I felt it. I wasn't panicky anymore. My crying stopped as if a dam had been shut down by the engineer. I got up off the sofa and brushed my hair back out of my face. I walked toward the door. I stepped outside. "Thank You, God."

The yard was still and quiet and very, very empty. I walked over to Mollie's house and shut the door. I picked up her dish, ball and old sock and took them to the shed. I emptied the water out of the wheelbarrow and put it away.

It was a strange experience walking through the yard alone. Mollie had always escorted me . . . to the garden, clothesline, birdbath . . . wherever. But now I walked slowly and victoriously over every inch of the yard. I felt as if I had been helped to win a great battle. Healing surely had begun in my broken heart.

Of course I still miss Mollie, but I am now able to recall the four years of happiness and intense love she brought to us. And I will always hold fast to the tremendous truth that I learned through losing her. God longs to be close to the broken-hearted. But He waits for us to cry out to Him. Then, regardless of what caused the pain, He responds to our deepest, our most desperate needs.

The Journey

CRYSTAL WARD KENT

When you bring a pet into your life, you begin a journey—a journey that will bring you more love and devotion than you have ever known, yet also test your strength and courage.

If you allow, the journey will teach you many things, about life, about yourself, and most of all, about love. You will come away changed forever, for one soul cannot touch another without leaving its mark.

Along the way, you will learn much about savoring life's simple pleasures—jumping in leaves, snoozing in the sun, the joy of puddles, and even the satisfaction of a good scratch behind the ears.

If you spend much time outside, you will be taught how to truly experience every element, for no rock, leaf or log will go unexamined, no rustling bush will be overlooked, and even the very air will be inhaled, pondered, and noted as being full of valuable information. Your pace may be slower—except when heading home to the food dish—but you will become a better naturalist, having been taught by an expert in the field.

Too many times we hike on automatic pilot, our goal being to complete the trail rather than enjoy the journey. We miss the details—the colorful mushrooms on the rotting log, the honeycomb in the old maple snag, the hawk feather caught on a twig. Once we walk as a dog does, we discover a whole new world. We stop; we browse the landscape; we kick over leaves, peek in tree holes, look up, down, all around. And we learn what any dog knows: that nature has created a marvelously complex world that is full of surprises, that each cycle of the seasons brings ever-changing wonders, each day an essence all its own.

Even from indoors you will find yourself more attuned to the world around you. You will find yourself watching summer insects collecting on a screen (How bizarre they are! How many kinds there are!), or noting the flick and flash of fireflies through the dark. You will stop to observe the swirling dance of windblown leaves, or sniff the air after a rain. It does not matter that there is no objective in this; the point is in the doing, in not letting life's most important details slip by.

You will find yourself doing silly things that your pet-less friends might not understand: spending thirty minutes in the grocery aisle looking for the cat food brand your feline *must* have, buying dog birthday treats, or driving around the block an extra time because your pet enjoys the ride. You will roll in the snow, wrestle with chewie toys, bounce little rubber balls till your eyes cross, and even run around the house trailing your bathrobe tie—with a cat in hot pursuit—all in the name of love.

Your house will become muddier and hairier. You will wear less dark clothing and buy more lint rollers. You may find dog biscuits in your pocket or purse, and feel the need to explain that an old plastic shopping bag adorns your living room rug because your cat loves the crinkly sound.

You will learn the true measure of love—the steadfast, undying kind that says, "It doesn't matter where we are or what we do, or how life treats us as long as we are together." Respect this always. It is the most precious gift any living soul can give another. You will not find it often among the human race.

And you will learn humility. The look in my dog's eyes often made me feel ashamed. Such joy and love at my presence. She saw not some flawed human who could be cross and stubborn, moody or rude, but only her wonderful companion. Or maybe she saw those things and dismissed them as mere human foibles, not worth considering, and so chose to love me anyway.

If you pay attention and learn well, when the journey is done, you will be not just a better person, but the person your pet always knew you to be—the one they were proud to call beloved friend.

I must caution you that this journey is not without pain. Like all paths of true love, the pain is part of loving. For as surely as the sun sets, one day your dear animal companion will follow a trail you cannot yet go down. And you will have to find the strength and love to let them go. A pet's time on earth is far too short—especially for those that love them. We borrow them, really, just for awhile, and during these brief years they are generous enough to give us all their love, every inch of their spirit and heart, until one day there is nothing left.

The cat that only yesterday was a kitten is all too soon old and frail and sleeping in the sun. The young pup of boundless energy wakes up stiff and lame, the muzzle now gray. Deep down we somehow always knew that this journey would end. We knew that if we gave our hearts they would be broken. But give them we must for it is all they ask in return. When the time comes, and the road curves ahead to a place we cannot see, we give one final gift and let them run on ahead—young and whole once more. "Godspeed, good friend," we say, until our journey comes full circle and our paths cross again.

ACKNOWLEDGMENTS

(continued from page ii)

"My Beloved Biddie" is from *A Dog Is Listening,* by Roger A. Caras. Copyright © 1992 by Roger Caras. Published by Simon & Schuster.

"Sunshine," by Nancy B. Gibbs, is used by permission of the author.

"Elegy for Diamond," by Trish Maharam, is from *Intimate Nature,* edited by Linda Hogan, Deena Metzger and Brenda Peterson. Copyright © 1998 by Brenda Peterson, Deena Metzger and Linda Hogan. Copyright © 1998 by Trish Maharam.

"Mission Accomplished," by Pat Waldron, is used by permission of the author.

"Ol' Spud," by James A. Nelson, is from *Dog & Kennel,* October 1999.

"The Quail Chorus" is from *The Avocado Drive Zoo,* by Earl Hamner. Copyright © 1997, 1999 by Earl Hamner. Published by Cumberland House Publishing, Inc.

A Note From the Editors

This original Guideposts series was created by the Book and Inspirational Media Division of the company that publishes *Guideposts,* a monthly magazine filled with true stories of people's adventures in faith. *Guideposts* is available by subscription. All you have to do is write to Guideposts, 39 Seminary Hill Road, Carmel, New York 10512. When you subscribe, each month you can count on receiving exciting new evidence of God's presence, His guidance and His limitless love for all of us.

Guideposts is also available on the Internet by accessing our home page on the World Wide Web at www.guideposts.org. Send prayer requests to our Monday morning Prayer Fellowship. Read stories from recent issues of our magazines, *Guideposts, Angels on Earth, Clarity, Guideposts for Kids* and *Guideposts for Teens,* and follow our popular book of daily devotionals, *Daily Guideposts.* Excerpts from some of our best-selling books are also available.